FINDING HESTER

FINDING HESTER

The incredible story of the
hidden woman whose love letters
changed World War Two in
OPERATION MINCEMEAT

MIRROR BOOKS

MB

MIRROR BOOKS

© Erin Edwards

1

Published in Great Britain and Ireland in 2025 by
Mirror Books, a Reach PLC business.

www.mirrorbooks.co.uk
@TheMirrorBooks

Print ISBN 9781917439138
eBook ISBN 9781917439145

Cover Design: Chris Collins
Editing and Production: Jo Sollis, Christine Costello

Photographic acknowledgements: Wycombe Abbey
School Archive, Reach plc, Finding Hester research team,
Charterhouse School Archive, National Archive, Westminster
School Archive, Jesus Copeiro and Winchester College
Archive, Jak Malone

Every effort has been made to trace copyright.
Any oversight will be rectified in future editions.

Printed and bound in Great Britain by
CPI Group (UK) Ltd, Croydon, CR0 4YY

MIX
Paper | Supporting
responsible forestry
FSC
www.fsc.org   FSC® C013604

For Hester,
who served her nation

and for Jak,
without whom, in so many ways, this book would not exist

CONTENTS

Foreword   9

Welcome To MI5   15
The Name Of A Hero   29
If It's Up, It's Up As One   39
Additional Research: Finding Charles   56
Making A Hero   68
Additional Research: Finding Ewen   83
Hester's Family   100
Finding Living Leggatts   111
Additional Research: Finding Haselden   125
Picture The Scene   137
Welcome To The British Government   146
Additional Research: Finding Averil   161
For Hester, Who Served Her Nation   173
Additional Research: Finding Watkins   185
The Box   203
Dear Val   220
Soon The Journey Will Be Done   252

Acknowledgements   263
Photos   267
Sources   275

FOREWORD

JAK MALONE

NEW YORK CITY, 1ST FEBRUARY 2025

**THREE WEEKS BEFORE OPERATION
MINCEMEAT DEBUTED ON BROADWAY**

IN sunny March of 2019, I travelled from my native Merseyside to London for a week of initial workshops for the first production of *Operation Mincemeat*, a new musical based on an obscure chapter of World War Two history. Our base of operations for the week was an eclectic re-hearsal space in East London called Theatre Deli, which offered (and, I believe, still does) cheap rehearsal spaces for folks who are creating new work. The rooms themselves were repurposed offices. For our first day, they stuck us in 'The Boardroom.' The group in the room next to us was emphatically rehearsing an opera, while the team on the other side was preparing a play for the Edinburgh Fringe Festival and could frequently be heard chanting, 'Down with the government!' It was here − sandwiched between the cacophony, cross-legged on the carpeted office floor – that I was first told the story of Operation Mincemeat.

'We'll start by laying out the story and how it all fits into a two-act musical.'

A flimsy whiteboard was dragged over, and a fresh pack of pens cracked open. I'd heard a few songs from the show and had done a cursory Google search, but I had more or less gone into this week blind.

The musical was being created by Spitlip, a four-headed monster of theatre makers whose work I had admired for years. Dave, Zoë, Tash, and Felix were creating work that spoke to me on a cellular level – clever-funny, seriously silly, often a bit gross, and always fast-paced and wordy. When they announced *Mincemeat*, I did absolutely nothing to hide my enthusiasm for the project, and after a couple of desperate auditions – I was in! I knew the show would be rooted in historical truth, but I also knew it was *their* show, and they'd do it *their* way. I was excited to hear them tell it.

What followed was a half-hour journey through 1940s wartime London, with a stop-off in Nazi-occupied Spain and a big Hollywood finish – told by three exceptional character actors and a maverick musician. It was a Looney Tunes-style fight cloud of ideas, plotlines, characters, and songs. I was completely riveted. In that little boardroom, I had a front-row seat to the first primitive showing of what I already knew was going to be my new favourite musical.

Operation Mincemeat itself is insane – an incredible story that I still have trouble believing myself. A group of plucky individuals who pull off the unthinkable – a moment in history that truly deserves to shine. I felt so excited that I got to tell this story, and I was even more thrilled when I learned how the show would be cast.

'There are five of us in it, and we'll play everybody.' And they meant that – hundreds of characters. Heroes, heroines, street urchins, pilots, admirals, waiters, secretaries, spies, and shoeshine boys. Everyone was up for grabs, regardless of race, gender or type. This was an exciting prospect for me – a habitual multi-roler who always chased the high that only came with well-executed shape-shifting. I left that morning rehearsal knowing two things. First, *this show is going to be a hit*. And second, *I want to play the secretary, Hester.*

It may come as a surprise to learn that my reasons for coveting the role of Hester had little to do with how remarkable her story was, or how qualified I felt to tell it. What actually drew me to the part was the logistics. I had rather cynically figured out that, because Hester was more of an outlier within the central plot and the five lead characters, landing the Hester track would likely give me more opportunity to play additional supporting roles. That would maximise the fun and give me scope to be more cartoonish, grotesque and stupid. I had listened closely to the story –I knew the creepy coroner, the inconvenient pilot, and the stoic submarine captain were all up for grabs – and I wanted to play them all. And, dear reader, that's exactly how it worked out.

The afternoon portion of rehearsal saw me taking on Hester's tragic love ballad, *Dear Bill*. I loved the song from the get-go. I found it remarkable – beautiful melody, exceptional lyrics. Reverent and conversational, with moments that make the heart stop. Both intimate and vast in scope. A magnum opus of quiet grief. And to know the song is to instantly know the character – restrained, practical, but incredibly sweet. Most wouldn't believe me when I say that approaching Hester came easily, but everyone knows someone like her. Someone who's no fun at all until you talk to them about the right thing and they bloom like a rose. All the pieces were there from the start, and most of them could be found in the song.

I performed *Dear Bill* that day in front of the cast, the writers, and our spirited lighting designer, Sherry, who, by the end of the song, was wiping away tears. That's how we knew we had something that worked. And with that, Hester was mine.

And, fortunately for me, that's how it stayed – at least for the next few years. The five-week run in the summer of 2019 was followed by a shorter run later that year. After a brief global pandemic, we returned for another run in a bigger theatre, followed by an extension, then yet another run – all leading up to London's West End. Each time I returned to the show, I'd put Hester on like a comfortable pair of slippers. And I'd miss her during the downtime. After all, her posture is so much better than mine.

The reaction to Hester was more than I ever could have hoped. People just *love* her. They so willingly see through her hardened exterior and love her for her dedication, her passion, and her old romantic heart. Some even come to the stage door to tell me things meant for Hester. I've had women tell me they see themselves represented in her, which is the highest possible compliment for a chubby little bloke who's just trying his best. Occasionally, I meet people who are bereaved or widowed, and they talk about the song – how it speaks to them. In those instances, there are often tears and always hugs.

For so many years, I felt like I was *her* secretary – the middleman, fielding an outpouring of affection for this historically enigmatic woman. When I landed the role, I did what little research I could to find out who she was. I was dismayed to find nothing. No photos, no dates, no records at all. It seemed she had been entirely forgotten. So I felt a tremendous duty to look after her – to do her justice and celebrate her for the vital work that she did. And for a long time, I felt that responsibility was mine alone.

Until one day, something remarkable happened.

I was idly scrolling through Twitter when I noticed a conversation on there that centred around…

…actually, you know what, I simply *must* let our brilliant

authors tell this one. They've done all this amazing work, and here I am prattling on. You're in for a treat. It's an incredible story that I still have trouble believing myself. A group of plucky individuals who pull off the unthinkable – a moment in history that truly deserves to shine. I'm wary of giving away spoilers, but I hope it's enough to say that I'm tremendously proud of and grateful to everyone involved.

It's hard to say what the real-life Hester would have made of all this. But what I *can* say with absolute certainty is that *my* Hester – the Hester with the roses, and the gin, and the complicated stamps – is quietly delighted. She told me to tell you that she loves her plaque and thinks you're all marvellous. But above all, she's extremely jealous of the vast amounts of admin you all got to do. She just did a little wiggle thinking about it.

CHAPTER ONE

WELCOME TO MI5

WHEN we first considered how best to start this book, it seemed like a simple summary of Operation Mincemeat itself might be a good bit of context to introduce the whole tale. That was our first mistake. There is no simple version of Operation Mincemeat. It is the perfect example of the phrase 'truth is stranger than fiction'. When writing group SpitLip started to preview the musical they were developing about this operation, they were frequently told to cut various details because no one would believe them. Even when these details were true.

It's understandable. Nothing about the 1943 plan seems sensible. Find a corpse, dress him up like a British pilot, and drop him in the sea off the coast of Huelva, Spain. Plant fake documents in his briefcase that discuss a fictitious plot to invade Sardinia, rather than Sicily as was actually planned, and hope those documents get intercepted by German spies active in Spain. And, to top it all off, equip the corpse with the usual objects a man might have with him, in an attempt to sell the ruse: cigarettes, an ID card, a photograph of a lover, receipts, ticket stubs, and letters. All carefully devised to illustrate a believable life.

It was a baffling plan. Even more strangely, it actually worked.

The German spies in Huelva intercepted the documents and passed them up the chain of command until they were in the hands of Adolf Hitler himself.

After the war, British intelligence services would recover confirmation that the information was believed to be real. The Germans began to focus more attention on Sardinia, the invasion of Sicily was a success, and the Allies ultimately won the war. And, over 70 years later, a group of four writer-performers wrote a musical about it.

At first glance it might seem like an odd concept for a musical, but this is an art form that brought us *Starlight Express* and *Sweeney Todd: The Demon Barber of Fleet Street*. *Les Misérables* is based on a 655,000 word novel with sizeable tangents about the French sewer system, and it's the longest running musical in the world. Sometimes the stranger the source material, the better the show, so perhaps this odd little war story was perfect.

Operation Mincemeat the musical has never had the budget of the mega-musicals of *Les Misérables'* era, though, and the cheapest way to put on a show is to pay the fewest number of people. SpitLip's *Operation Mincemeat* has a cast of five. They multi-role throughout the show, all playing as many characters as necessary, but they each have one main role.

There's Ewen Montagu, a self-proclaimed genius Naval Intelligence agent with cloying charisma; Charles Cholmondeley, who dreams up the operation with quiet brilliance; Johnny Bevan, the colonel who has the misfortune to be in charge of the team; Jean Leslie, a young typing girl keen to make something of herself; and Hester Leggett, a matronly, long-suffering secretary who comes across as efficient but uptight in equal measure.

All the characters are based on real people involved in the operation, sharing their names and their roles and, where possible, their characteristics. Things are overplayed for comic effect, of course, but they are rooted in reality. For Hester, however, the gaps that needed to be filled with fictionalised content were wider than with the others.

The seminal book on Operation Mincemeat is Ben Macintyre's *Operation Mincemeat: The True Spy Story That Changed the Course of World War Two*. Before its publication in 2010, the author was able to interview former MI5 secretary Jean Leslie. A photograph of Jean at the beach was included in the briefcase sent to Huelva, making her the face of 'Pam', the pilot's fictitious fiancée. In her interview, Jean recalled that one of the women responsible for writing two love letters by 'Pam' was Hester Leggett, another MI5 employee who oversaw the secretarial unit with draconian authority. This was the first recognition of Hester in the public eye, but other than Jean's recollections, little else was known about her.

With almost nothing to go on, including Hester in retellings of the Operation Mincemeat story required a significant amount of creative interpretation. In the eponymous 2021 film, she's an older woman in her 70s who worked as a private secretary for Montagu before he takes on a role with Naval Intelligence. She gets her job at MI5 only because she moves to the organisation with him. In the epilogue of the film, they claim she stayed on as the Director of the Admiralty Secretarial Unit, although it's unclear where exactly this information comes from.

When SpitLip, a writing group formed of David Cumming, Felix Hagan, Natasha Hodgson and Zoë Roberts, began tackling a musical of Operation Mincemeat, they immediately realised the story was lacking in female characters, so including the few women already attached to the tale was an obvious choice, making sure their roles were told. Women working at MI5 during the war outnumbered their male colleagues and leaving them out didn't seem right, even if their jobs weren't the kind that provided them with any real power at the organisation. They still had stories to tell.

SpitLip were already less than pleased to find themselves

writing a musical about World War Two. As far as they were concerned, it had been done before enough times to render it overworked, but they knew they wanted to adapt something or tell a true story. After a string of plays that were containing increasing amounts of music, this was their first official musical, and they were keen not to make the process more difficult for themselves by having to start from scratch.

It was while they were on the hunt for the perfect source material that Natasha's brother, a vet and not a theatre writer, suggested she consider a podcast he'd been listening to. She was initially apprehensive to take recommendations from him, because everyone always thinks they have the next great idea when they don't have to be the one to actually write it, and what do vets know about writing musicals anyway. Eventually she relented and listened to the podcast, before begrudgingly calling up the rest of SpitLip and telling them they were all going to have to write a musical about World War Two. Operation Mincemeat was simply too weird and wonderful a concept to pass up.

The musical developed through a series of writing sessions and scratch nights, with some early songs still in the show today and others ending up on the cutting room floor. They had to condense a complicated military operation into something that made sense in two and half hours, with a limited cast, the barest suggestion of a set, and a costume department consisting almost solely of a box of old hats. Luckily, SpitLip were, well, old hats at creating a show on a budget. They had each person playing dozens of roles over the course of the show, indicating the character changes with a change of glasses or ties, or a simple spin around to show a different facial expression.

Still, they needed more actors than just themselves on stage. They'd been swapping roles around between themselves so far, with Natasha playing Hester at a scratch night to preview some songs, and old YouTube videos showing Felix taking on the role of Montagu, but it was time to hold auditions. They'd secured a slot to perform the show at the New Diorama Theatre in Camden in 2019 and they couldn't quite manage all the characters they'd created by themselves.

Their official first cast ended up consisting of Natasha, Zoë, and David from SpitLip (with Felix taking on a musical director role), and newcomers Jak Malone and Rory Furey-King. When they held auditions, they knew they were looking for two additions, but no specific characters had yet been allocated. Jak recalls being asked to perform a song as a woman as part of his audition, however, so the idea of him playing Hester had already been considered. Sure enough, on the first day of rehearsals, after Jak had sung Hester's song *Dear Bill* for the first time, roles were assigned and the long list of characters he would be playing throughout the show was crowned with Hester's name.

With so little source material to go on, SpitLip's version of Hester was largely their own creation, drawing on the two concrete things that the real Jean Leslie remembered about her: that she was a spinster, and Jean had perceived her as embittered. SpitLip made their Hester 49, old enough to have experienced World War One as a young woman. It was a fair assumption, based on the scant knowledge that she was the most senior woman in the department and with Jean's specific memory of her as unmarried. The memory of her being bitter found its way into the show through Hester's disapproval of Jean's informal interruptions of her superiors and disliking her overly loud enthusiasm. Hester is a stickler for the rules and doing things the right way, her no-nonsense and dependable nature admired, or at least respected, by the other members of the team. Even if Jean finds her old-fashioned demeanour a little exasperating when it clashes with her ideas of female empowerment and a woman's right to a place in the workforce.

SpitLip didn't leave her as a bitter spinster with no development, however. A crucial part of Hester's character is her experience losing a lover in World War One. It's a loss she suppresses until her emotional song near the end of Act One, *Dear Bill*, where the audience, and Jean, see a new side to her. The song is one of the few moments of the show that has remained almost entirely unchanged since the early days of development.

During the 2020 Covid-19 national lockdown, SpitLip released a live recording of the song from the New Diorama Theatre run on the website Soundcloud. In the description, they shared that they had not planned on releasing a song from a show still in development, but wanted those separated from their loved ones to feel less alone. Despite their hesitance to share it, the lyrics remain unchanged in the version of the show that made it to the West End. When Jak listens back to it, the only difference he hears is in how it's performed. Back in 2019, he focused more on getting the technical aspects of the song right. By the time he concluded his year-long West End run as Hester, the song was less polished and more human, with more of Hester's character in the performance, even if that meant sacrificing technical perfection.

For Jak, *Dear Bill* was the only part of the show that felt like work. It's so different tonally from the rest of the show, with all the focus on Hester, and the length of the song came with a constant risk of forgetting the words, something he thankfully never did. The responsibility of carrying the emotional weight of the show was not something to be taken lightly, and any and all backstage – or on stage – hijinks had to be postponed at least until after *Dear Bill* had been successfully delivered.

The song has since been performed by Christian

Andrews, who took over the role of Hester in the second year of the West End show, at the Royal Albert Hall during a concert to mark the 80th anniversary of D-Day. In the show, it's a moment of calm in frantic chaos and it stands as an explanation for Hester's bitterness. In it, she recalls writing love letters to a man deployed overseas in World War One, before he lost his life. In SpitLip's interpretation of the character, she is unmarried because she lost the love of her life, and she is embittered because she is suppressing overwhelming feelings of loss that are coming to the surface once again as another war wages on around her. Their Hester channels her own experience of writing love letters to a soldier into the letters she writes to add authenticity to the pilot created for the operation, despite the emotional cost of re-experiencing her grief. When *Dear Bill* is performed, it is often to an accompaniment of sniffles and tears supplied by the audience.

When Jak took Hester on, he developed the role with inspirations from his grandmother and his former head-teacher, eager to make her formidable but very human, peppering in her enthusiasm for rubber stamps and the card game bridge. Her costume is a shirt, trousers and a pair of glasses on a chain, all kept relatively simple to allow for quick changes in and out of other characters by swapping accessories.

Despite the limitations of the costume, Jak imagines

Hester immaculately dressed, with starched clothes and new shoes, and without a hair out of place. On stage, the only viable way to represent this imagined hairstyle was with a single curl, teased out and gelled down to the forehead to keep it in place for the entire show. It's a detail Jak added before the first show at the New Diorama, wanting to hint at his vision for Hester's look. It became an iconic and integral part of the character, now sported by whoever is playing her. Jak sometimes regretted his decision, when keeping it in check required half a bottle of hairspray, but those familiar with the character now can't imagine her without that curl.

It has always been the plan to have Hester as the kind of character that you think would be one thing, but is then revealed to be another, and Jak had been part of creating her in a collaborative process with SpitLip. The group hadn't yet hired a director, so were bouncing ideas off each other, and Jak remembers the rehearsal process as the most fun he'd ever had in his life. He embraced Hester's 'hard to love' nature and the underlying lovability and humour behind her once her exterior was cracked. When he went on stage at the New Diorama Theatre that first night, Hester felt like his character. He trusted SpitLip's work, already familiar with them before *Operation Mincemeat,* and believed that the audience would be receptive to their work and what they were trying to do with the characters.

The gender-bending of *Operation Mincemeat* doesn't stop with Hester. Ewen Montagu, who fancies himself the main character of the ensemble piece, was initially played by Natasha, and Zoë took on the role of Johnny Bevan. The division of secondary and tertiary characters has no consideration for gender whatsoever, with each part, be it German spy or MI5 typing pool girl, going to whoever was free to play it in that scene. It's never intended to be a comical decision. Rather than akin to a pantomime dame – a part often played for laughs – it's more comparable to the role of the principal boy being a female part. Peter Pan is historically played by a woman for reasons of practicality: the character needs to look young enough to be a child and be light enough to easily rig with wires for flight scenes. Ewen Montagu is played by a woman because if he were played by a man, he would be so incredibly insufferable that the entire show would fall apart. His overconfident bravado in the hands of the women who have played him thus far instead comes across as charming, and a send-up of an entitled, public school alumni brand of patriarchy, rather than support of it.

Hester being played by a man is a little more subtle, but equally works to chip away at gender roles throughout the show. It's not often that a man gets to stand on stage and openly grieve a lost lover and giving Jak, and all subsequent Hester actors, the most emotional song of the piece creates a rare space for male vulnerability. It's a part of the show the writers are keen to protect: the script specifies that gender is irrelevant to casting, with the exception of Ewen and Hester, who must be played by a female-identifying actor and a male-identifying actor respectively.

The weird but wonderful show SpitLip put together was a hit at the New Diorama Theatre for a month from mid-May to mid-June in 2019. In January of 2020, the show played another short run at the Southwark Playhouse in Elephant and Castle. Claire-Marie Hall took over the role of Jean Leslie, completing a cast line-up that would eventually become the original West End principal cast.

Despite Covid-19 scuppering some plans, a further Southwark Playhouse run followed in 2021, and another in 2022. Enthusiastic word of mouth saw to it that performances were selling out. The show was tweaked and edited between runs, and sometimes during them, but the soul of the piece that resonated with audiences and early reviewers didn't change.

By this point, the show had found its core cast and was keen not to let them go, and the cast was equally keen to stay attached to the project. Jak Malone will admit that he deliberately made Hester difficult for anyone else to play, the threat of being dispensed with in favour of stunt casting a worry in the back of his mind. His entire arsenal is in the show – every accent, every character, every curl. He needn't have worried – the role was always his to come back to, and he deliberately stayed free for the show's return.

In 2022, the show moved to Riverside Studios in Hammersmith for a run of almost three months, picking up an additional cast member on the way. David, who had been playing the role of Charles Cholmondeley, was injured in a bike accident days before previews were due to begin. Last minute replacement Seán Carey had 10 days to learn the role before the show's delayed opening. When the show finally moved to the West End, Seán went with it as part of their new group of understudies, joined by Geri Allen, Holly Sumpton, and Christian Andrews. It was Christian who would understudy the role of Hester, with Seán in line as second cover. Both men would play her multiple times over the initial year-long contract, each perfecting the signature Hester curl.

The long-awaited first West End preview of the show was on the 31st of March 2023, at the 432-seat Fortune Theatre. Director Robert Hastie greeted an enthusiastic audience and announced that he knew there were plenty of people in the audience who were new to the show, at which point he was drowned out by a wave of laughter. Almost everyone there that night had seen it at least once before, and would see it at least once again. It's just that kind of show.

Scattered throughout the audience, most of us not yet having met, were many of the people who would go on to find the real Hester. We were all there because we were drawn to this madcap story of five people who made a difference, albeit in the weirdest way possible. It never occurred to any of us at that point that we might become part of the show's story.

CHAPTER TWO

THE NAME OF A HERO

THE typical invested *Operation Mincemeat* fan is fairly young, probably in their twenties, and female. There's also an interestingly high rate of neurodiversity and queerness among our legions, which likely speaks to depictions of characters that have been interpreted to also be neurodiverse, and the gender-bent casting, which appeals to a queer audience in its rejection of gender norms.

The typical member of what became Team #FindingHester doesn't really exist. We're a motley crew of varying ages, certainly skewing older than the average fan, and from a wide variety of career paths. We have educators, lawyers, archivists, authors, doctoral researchers, marketers, technologists, and many more represented in our ranks. The vast majority of us reside in England, but we would also gain additional members from across the pond in America as our research efforts developed.

Our experiences of finding out about the musical, coming to love it, and being drawn to the research efforts are equally as varied, as the perspectives of three members of the team show:

CLAUDIA CAPLAN WOLFF

My journey to *Operation Mincemeat* was an unusual one that started in 2022 at Huelva, Spain at the grave of Glyndwr Michael, the real name of the man whose corpse was used in the operation. As an avid reader of Ben Macintyre's work, I had read his book about Operation Mincemeat years before. I always felt a personal connection to the story because my husband's sister has lived in Huelva for many years. We live on the East Coast of the U.S. and had originally planned to go to Huelva for a visit in the summer of 2020, but of course, everything shut down because of Covid-19. Finally, in May of 2022, we were able to travel to Europe. One of our goals was to visit Nuestra Señora de la Soledad Cemetery.

My sister-in-law grew up in London and when we mentioned to her that we were going to the grave, she told us that a friend of hers in London had seen a musical about Operation Mincemeat and loved it. A musical? We were incredulous to say the least. I looked up the reviews and it certainly seemed promising. We were on our way back to London, so we bought tickets to see the show at Riverside Studios – quite a long tube ride from where we were staying in Shoreditch.

Needless to say, we were amazed, moved and charmed by the show. After it was over, we waited for the cast to come out to tell them how much we enjoyed the performance and that we were sure they were destined for the West End. When we showed Claire the pictures of the grave, she started to cry. We felt an immediate connection with all of them.

When I then saw the beginnings of the #FindingHester project online, I decided to get involved and apply the research techniques I used as a history major at Columbia University to assist in the research.

ANNABEL ROSE

I first heard about *Operation Mincemeat* from a friend who saw its first full run at New Diorama Theatre – and I'm still a bit jealous of her now. She messaged me to say it was on at Southwark Playhouse and I absolutely had to see it.

I managed to get tickets, and in February 2022 I immediately fell in love with the show. It was the perfect example of, for me, so many of the things that make theatre so special – witty lyrics, beautiful melodies that really make your brain tingle, a talented cast, and motifs and layers of meaning you can read into (if that's your idea of fun).

I saw the show again at Riverside Studios and booked again for the preview period as soon as the West End run was announced. At the time, this felt so extravagant – seeing the same show three times was almost unheard of for me.

The character of Hester has always been particularly special to me – I could write (and have written) pages and pages about her. SpitLip and Jak Malone crafted such a beautiful character, who has such delicate depth. I've seen the show a lot of times now, and yet every single time it's still such a privilege to see Hester gradually find space and safety to open up and find a sense of community with the other characters.

I always wondered about the 'real' Hester – and found it sad that she didn't seem to be known or remembered in the same way as some of the people behind the other characters.

I first saw #FindingHester on Twitter – and burst into tears! I wasn't initially sure about getting involved, because I didn't have any relevant experience or skills, but I was welcomed into the online community and attempted to do my bit.

It's been a whirlwind from there. I've never been the kind of person to recreate a character's costume, join online fan communities, or make fanart – but *Operation Mincemeat* (and the character of Hester) changed all that.

I have a lot of treasured memories from the show but –

without wanting to spoil the book you're reading – being dressed as the character of Hester (complete with the iconic forehead curl) while hearing of a letter and, later, opening a box are two of the most special.

I feel utterly privileged to have been involved in the whole adventure, and I'm really grateful to my friends for working so hard to find Hester and make sure her story is told.

ERIN EDWARDS

Unfortunately, the early New Diorama Theatre run of *Operation Mincemeat* passed me by and remains one of the theatrical experiences I most regret missing out on. I was, however, lucky enough to be living within walking distance of Southwark Playhouse when the show started its runs there. I've always been a history nerd and I've been a musical theatre fan for well over a decade, so a history musical just around the corner was a guaranteed booked ticket for me.

The Southwark Playhouse is an excellent off-West End venue that has put out some incredible shows, so my hopes were high. I'd first heard of Operation Mincemeat in vague terms on the BBC television show *QI*, with it receiving a fairly short cameo in Series K in 2013. Still, even the rough sketch of a corpse being dressed up like a pilot and thrown in the sea was strange enough that it stuck with me. Even if I'd had the full story beforehand, however, it still wouldn't have prepared me for what unfolded on that stage.

It was immediately clear that this show was something special. I've seen hundreds of shows that would fall up and down a sliding scale of excellence, but sometimes there are productions that you just immediately know will go far. *Operation Mincemeat* was the perfect blend of humour, history, talent and, all-important for a musical, memorable songs. With a small cast and an intimate venue, it felt like the audience was in on the joke the whole way through. The cast was working extremely hard, running from wing to wing to play their lengthy roster of characters, before belting out some of the best songs I'd ever heard in a fringe theatre.

It seemed impossible that this show wouldn't make it to the West End but, just in case, I kept going back. Sometimes I took friends, unafraid anyone I introduced to it wouldn't like it, and sometimes I booked solo trips. It probably got to a point where the ushers at the theatre recognised me, but if they did, they were good enough not to mention it.

Part of my fondness for the show came from the fact that I worked for an organisation that had ties to the real Ewen Montagu, and I was pleased to see one of our alumni represented on stage. Seeing the show encouraged me to do some more digging into him at work and I came across a listing for him on a website that records burial sites of individuals internationally. For some reason, I thought to double check the information on the page, and found it was wrong. What followed was a lengthy search to correct it, contacting cemeteries across London and eventually getting in touch with his family to clarify the situation so I could write to the website and remove the incorrect place of burial. A boring, and potentially pointless, task for many, but I greatly enjoyed the satisfaction of having set the record straight.

While I was poking around on the Find a Grave website, I found myself typing in the names of the other individuals represented in the show. Charles Cholmondeley was there, but Jean Leslie and Hester Leggett weren't. This struck me as particularly sad, since both these female characters in the musical sing about the lack of legacy they expect to leave. It was disappointing that it turned out they were right.

I never did find Jean Leslie's grave, but there is a fair amount of information about her online. Her obituary was featured in *The Telegraph* in 2012, when she passed away at the age of 88. Later in life she had publicly spoken about her role in Operation Mincemeat, and of course been interviewed on the subject.

There was nothing on Hester. Nothing at all besides the mentions in Ben Macintyre's book, which I had by then read cover to cover and annotated with Post-it Notes. Not only was there no mention of her burial site, there was no mention of anyone by that name existing at the right time. I searched for her on family history research sites and couldn't come up with a date of birth or a date of death. One of the first things you realise when doing historical research on individuals is the variance in the spelling of names, especially surnames. By the 20th century, this was rarely the problem it had been further back in time, but on the off-chance, I tried a few different spellings. I came up with two potential Hester Leggatts who were alive and living in London during World War Two. I jotted their names down on a red note card and kept it on my desk for over two years.

In April 2022, Jak Malone tweeted about not being able to find a picture of Hester Leggett and I replied with my theory about the misspelling of Leggatt, adding that I'd yet to find time to visit the National Archives or write to MI5 to check. I promised myself I would do more research, but finding that necessary time and having the resources to access material behind a paywall wasn't something I was able to do until a wider group committed themselves to the task.

****

As the spotlight on the *Operation Mincemeat* musical grew during their time on West End, the fans had questions about the real figures behind the characters. In June 2023, someone reached out to SpitLip on Twitter to ask whether the real Hester had lost someone in World War One, like she does in the show. SpitLip tweeted back with an explanation of the lack of information:

Really sadly we could find very little information about the real Hester – according to the history books she's not a figure that matters much – which made us all the more determined to make the world fall in love with her

It was never meant to be a challenge, or a call to action to spark a research project, but they had quoted the tweet with their response, which posted it to the timelines of their followers, so a challenge it became. And it didn't take long for the community to start supplying results.

With no evidence of a Hester Leggett to be found, a misspelling was the obvious answer, and there were two Hester Leggatts that seemed like a potential match: Hester Kate Leggatt, and Hester May Murray Leggatt. Both lived in London during World War Two, so on the surface either could have been 'our' Hester. However, there was one thing we could say about Hester for sure, one thing Jean Leslie remembered for over 60 years: Hester wasn't married. Hester Kate Leggatt had married into the surname before the start of the war, which meant she couldn't be the Hester we were searching for.

That left Hester May Murray Leggatt.

It wasn't quite as easy as saying we had successfully identified Hester at this stage. There were a few other less likely, but not entirely impossible, matches, and there was no guarantee that 'Leggatt' was the correct spelling of Hester's surname at all. And considering one identified error with the misspelling, we could not even be completely certain that everything else was true. Maybe our Hester wasn't even a spinster. Still, it was something to start from. If we couldn't prove Hester M.M. Leggatt was the right Hester, perhaps we would be able to rule her out, and move on to someone else.

The Twitter thread started by SpitLip's tweet quickly became an uncontrollable, and unfollowable, cacophony of voices as multiple people chimed in to provide matches for Hester in various family history tools they had access to. It was complete chaos but it was extraordinary to watch as it unfolded. You couldn't look away from the screen for more than a few minutes without having a dozen new messages to catch up on, all throwing out ideas for new ways to investigate. If this was what was possible in an informal, disorganised way, the potential of success for a dedicated research project was tangible.

In a matter of hours, more had been done to find Hester than had been done in the entire history of Operation Mincemeat research.

And we were only just beginning.

CHAPTER THREE

IF IT'S UP, IT'S UP
AS ONE

WITH the most likely match for Operation Mincemeat's Hester identified, there were seemingly endless avenues of research that could be followed. In many ways, Hester May Murray Leggatt was the perfect person to research. We would go on to learn that she was ideally placed to leave behind a substantial archival footprint, attending the right school, occupying the right social class, and living at the right time to ensure her appearance in a wealth of documents.

She had also been deemed unimportant enough to go unresearched for as long as she did, leaving all those documents as yet undiscovered. Mapping the life story of Hester Leggatt might have been a lengthy and involved project, but discovering Hester Leggett didn't exist had been a simple task, accomplished in little more than one census search. The most important step we took was in deciding that Hester mattered, and that fuelled the initial frenzy of research.

Before we could do much else, we needed to establish the core details of Hester's life. Once we had her dates of birth and death and the names of her parents, we would have a list of information that future potential finds could be compared against to ensure we were on the right track and looking at the right person. The potential to tangle ourselves up with records for Hester Kate Leggatt was a real risk.

One of the easiest documents to use to start to research these fundamental details of someone's life is a census. They provide full names, ages and occupations of all individuals living in the country, and often family connections can also be gleaned from those living in the same household. People also like to add in their pets, despite that being against the rules. Listed in the 1921 Census of England and Wales are seven horses, 17 dogs, 144 cats, three goldfinches, seven chickens, one rooster, one tortoise… and one Hester Leggatt.

The census shows Hester as a 15-year-old schoolgirl at Wycombe Abbey School in Surrey. As she was living in a boarding house at the school rather than with her family, her parents and any potential siblings were not immediately evident, but we did get another standard piece of census data in her place of birth: Karachi, India.

Located in what is now Pakistan, Karachi was under British control when Hester was born there in 1905. Her father worked as a judge in the Indian Civil Service and the family was mostly based in India, although participated in the common practice of sending children back to England to attend boarding school.

Hester attended Wycombe Abbey and her two brothers, we would later come to learn, attended Charterhouse and Winchester College. Hester was certainly not the only British child born in India who was attending Wycombe Abbey. Even on the same page of the 1921 Census form that features her name, there is the name of another pupil born in Darjeeling, India, specifying in the next column across that she was also born to British parents.

The initial planned date for the 1921 Census was in April, but the civil unrest of Black Friday, which saw transport and rail unions fail to call for strike action in support of miners, pushed the date back to 19th June 1921. Thankfully, this new date also fell during the school term, capturing the name of Hester's school in the Census response. Had it been pushed back into the school holidays, we might have lost what would turn out to be a vital lead.

There is no mention of Hester in the 1911 census, suggesting she was still in India with her parents, not yet old enough to have been attending school, but both brothers were boarding at Parkside School in Ewell, Surrey at this time. They were close in age, born only one year apart, but Hester was five years younger and the only girl. It can be assumed that she didn't see much of them growing up, with them often in different countries. It was not quick or easy to travel between India and England, so it is unlikely that the journey was made regularly.

Hester's birthplace being India made the job of researching her very early life slightly more complicated. We have never been able to locate her birth certificate but, in the absence of one, the British India Office Birth and Baptism records provided her exact date of birth as 20th December 1905, in the record for her baptism on 26th January 1906. It also lists the names of her parents: Ernest Hugh Every Leggatt and Jessie Leggatt, whose maiden name, Murray, became one of Hester's middle names.

Both of Hester's parents came from British families based in India. Her father was born in 1870 in the Chingleput district, in the north east of the country, and her mother was born in Bombay in 1874. Ernest Leggatt was educated at St Paul's School, demonstrating the practice of a British boarding education that he would adopt for all three of his children. He passed away in 1935 in Devon, having relocated to England.

Jessie Leggatt was one of four children, all daughters and all born in India. Ernest and Jessie split their time between India and England over the years, but do not always seem to have been living together. In the 1901

Census, she is living in Notting Hill, but Ernest appears to still be in India. It is unclear where Hester and her brothers were spending their school holidays from their respective boarding schools. Many pupils in similar circumstances would not have made the long journey back to family abroad and instead stayed with relatives or family friends in the United Kingdom. However, if Jessie was spending more of her time in the UK, it is possible she was doing so in order to be closer to her children out of term time.

In identifying Hester's birthday to be 20th December 1905, it takes only a simple sum to calculate her age in April 1943 when she worked on Operation Mincemeat. She was 37 years old. Far from Jean Leslie's recollections and the 2021 film's portrayal, we had found a woman who had worked hard to become relatively senior in her work at a fairly young age.

Since her name was first attached to the operation, Hester has been conceptualised with a focus almost entirely on her identity as a spinster. It is one of the few defining characteristics Jean Leslie recalled when discussing their time working together, and therefore it formed a signifi-cant part of the little we knew about Hester prior to 2023. Dramatisations of Hester were therefore built around this. An unmarried woman of 37 in 1943 could likely have expected to be referred to by the label of spinster, but the notion of her being beyond marrying age has translated into her being represented in modern adaptations of the story as far older than she really was. SpitLip made her 49, closer to her actual age, but the 2021 film places her in her 70s, roughly double the real Hester's age.

Jean Leslie was 19 when she worked on Operation Mincemeat in 1943, and she married only three years later. She, like many young women of the time, likely had marriage and motherhood as core goals in her life, perhaps even hoping to accomplish them by a specific age. When considering how she must have viewed Hester, who was almost double her age and unmarried, Leslie's memory of her as a spinster is understandable. Perhaps she never actually knew how old Hester was, but simply viewed her as old in comparison to herself, particularly with the potential for details to get blurred during the almost 70 years between her time at MI5 and her interview with Ben Macintyre.

It is also possible Leslie held a degree of judgement for a woman who had continued to work rather than keep a household for a husband, and this characterisation persisted in her memory. Or perhaps the label was not intended to be an insult, simply a factual description. Until 2005, it was a term used in UK law.

Today, spinster is considered more of a derogatory term. The male equivalent, bachelor, is often preceded by the adjective 'eligible', but there is never a notion of an 'eligible spinster'. In an effort to not pass judgement upon women based on their marital status, it has fallen out of fashion. The changing expectations for women may have shifted since 1943, but Hester's label of spinster has endured and led to her being misrepresented in the eyes of modern audiences. With new evidence of Hester's age, our perceptions of her started to shift. The image of her as a loveless, elderly spinster was clearly inaccurate, but we would have to wait to find out just how inaccurate.

The fairly recent date of death we uncovered for Hester further added to our surprise, with the span of her life overlapping with that of most of our researchers. To know that many of us had been born before she died only served to remind us of how recent this history was, yet it had already been misremembered and was in danger of staying that way. The sense of duty to correct the record felt all the heavier. It was also the first moment that we began to consider the possibility of living relatives who might remember Hester.

Hester passed away 4th August 1995 at the age of 89, never having spoken publicly about her role in Operation Mincemeat. We would later learn she had never discussed it with her family, either. It would be only 15 years after she died that Ben Macintyre's book was published, but her silence regarding her war work meant there was already no one aware of the connection who could correct the spelling of her surname. With the incorrect vowel making further research into a non-existent Hester Leggett impossible, she became a footnote to the Operation Mincemeat story.

With the core details of Hester's life established, each record that was uncovered was providing new pieces of information that could be followed up. Tweets were still pouring in with new revelations or potential identifications from different sources, but the lack of an organised approach meant multiple people were conducting the same searches and some details and links were going unnoticed. What had started as one initial thread had branched out into an unwieldly tangle of notifications and tags. The momentum and enthusiasm was impressive, but it very quickly became clear that we needed some structure to keep track of everything if we wanted to be efficient and accurate.

The goal from the start was to prove that we had found the right Hester. It felt wrong to allow the continued misspelling of her name in a musical that carried the message of accurately acknowledging everyone who contributed to Operation Mincemeat. The initial hope was that we might be able to convince the show to change her name in the programme and on their website, if we had enough evidence to make the case that Hester May Murray Leggatt was indeed the MI5 secretary who had helped to write the love letters that travelled with 'Bill' to Spain.

There was never a plan to write this book, nor to end up on the news, nor even, at this point, to track down her living family members. We had all begun this research because Hester had come to mean something to us, even if the Hester that we saw on stage was getting further and further away from the real Hester with each new piece of information.

The sentiment behind the musical's Hester still had an impact: she didn't do her work for fame, for medals or for glory, but because it was useful. It all contributed towards the war effort, and to trying to minimise the casualties amongst the Allied soldiers invading Sicily as much as was possible. SpitLip's Hester was happy just knowing she got the job done, but we wanted something more for the real Hester. Correcting her name in the historical record seems like such a minor thing, but we felt she deserved at least that. And in order to politely petition the show to change their character's name, we had to prove what we believed: that we had found Hester. To do that, we knew we had to be meticulous about our evidence.

The first thing that was set up was an online document that listed everything we found. This evolved into a very comprehensive record with footnotes, timelines and sources, but it began as simply somewhere to note each piece of information so it could all be tied together. When a potential new piece of the puzzle was discovered, it could be compared to what we already knew. Often this helped us confirm new finds, but it also helped us disprove others. The name 'Hester Leggatt' appears in a 1965 book entitled *The Handbook for Flower Arrangers*, crediting her with one of the floral arrangements featured, but also specifying a location of Southgate. There would have been a nice sense of serendipity to the real Hester taking an interest in flowers, since it is a motif used in the musical, but our timeline of Hester's life positioned her in Kensington.

Further research allowed us to identify the owner of the floral arrangement as Hester Kate Leggatt. The timeline document was an invaluable resource in keeping our Hesters straight and confirming whether each reference we found was to 'our' Hester. Thankfully, the majority were.

While our online document worked to record what we discovered, it was less well suited to hosting the collaborative research aspect of the project we'd all gotten involved in. Twitter had served an excellent purpose of pulling together a group of interested and engaged researchers, but the team we ended up with was large and somewhat amorphous. It was evident to everyone that we needed to move somewhere more organised, and where we'd be less of a nuisance, since SpitLip and Jak Malone undoubtedly wouldn't appreciate being constantly tagged in thousands of tweets about Hester research over a span of months.

What was also notable was the lack of a leader. From the start, this was a collaborative project and no one stepped forward to enforce any particular rule. Perhaps we would have been more efficient or more effective with someone in charge, handing out roles and tasks, but it never occurred to anyone as a position that needed filling. The strength of the project was in its adaptability and its creative use of the strengths of members of the team, organically settling into something that worked exactly as we needed. If someone had gotten as far as they could down a line of inquiry, someone else could either take it further or branch off what had already been discovered. There was no need to wait for approval or for tasks to be allocated.

But the lack of direct leadership did mean that no one stepped forward to start any kind of group chat. Doing so would have turned a voluntary research project into an invitation-only affair, undoubtedly excluding people who had plenty to add to the conversation. It would have also meant any developments in the research – and there were still plenty to come – would have been shared only in the privacy of the group. There were already so many people interested in Hester and we were excited to share our ongoing discoveries with an invested audience. With all of this in mind, we made the move to a Discord server.

Discord is an instant messaging social media platform that was initially built with gamers in mind, consisting of individual servers used for group discussion. Server owners can create a structure of different chat rooms, referred to as channels, that allow for multiple, organised conversations to take place in line with the topic of each channel. The platform has been adopted by a wide range of communities, including groups of theatre fans, and there was already an *Operation Mincemeat* server that a few researchers were a part of: the 'Mincefluencer' Discord.

Fans of the *Operation Mincemeat* musical commonly refer to themselves by this term (a portmanteau of 'Mincemeat' and 'influencers'), and the fan community around the show had been building since its first full run at the New Diorama Theatre in 2019, and during subsequent productions.

The name 'Mincefluencers' reflects the roots of the community, with people often seeing the show themselves and then telling a friend, or several friends, and 'influencing' them to go and see the production for themselves. It is a musical people can't help but talk about, both because it is good and because it is absolutely mad. Operation Mincemeat itself is a caper that doesn't quite seem real, and its retelling as a musical only heightens the baffling nature of the story. If it wasn't a case of convincing someone to go and see the show based on the merit of its genius, it was an assurance that you really had to see it to believe it. The word-of-mouth advertising was a powerful tool during its early runs.

The New Diorama Theatre run of the show was short and small, at just over four weeks long and playing to an audience of around 80 people. It was during the multiple runs at the slightly larger Southwark Playhouse that the musical found its audience. They waited patiently through the months that theatres were dark during the Covid-19 pandemic, and followed the show to Riverside Studios, where the first Mincefluencer pin badges were made to allow fans of the show to identify each other at performances. When it opened on the West End, the foundations of the fandom were already firmly established. It is now a show with a very enthusiastic fanbase, but the Discord server was, when we made the move there, fairly quiet. This wouldn't last.

A specific text chat channel was set up in the server for the #FindingHester project and we quickly migrated over to this space, filling it with our current research and new suggestions. Joining the server required having access to an invitation link, but that had always been freely given on Twitter to any potential Mincefluencers, so there was no barrier to access. Anyone willing to make a Discord account was welcome to join and continue the search for Hester in a slightly more organised manner.

Undoubtedly, we lost some people in this move. There were some individuals showing casual interest on Twitter, many of whom were simply spectating, but some were engaging in research of their own, and it is unlikely that all of them were willing to learn to navigate what may have been an entirely new social media platform just for this project. What we were left with, however, was a team of involved researchers who were willing to dedicate their time and pool their resources to see just how much of

Hester was out there to be found. At this point, we had no idea whether we would be able to dig up a huge amount more, or if we would soon start to hit dead ends, but there were plenty of avenues we wanted to try.

Once it became clear that there was also research that could be done into some of the other figures attached to Operation Mincemeat, a series of related channels were created. Discord channel names are all lowercase and preceded by a hash sign and soon enough the sidebar of the server was filled with a list of similar names: #find-ewen, for research into Lieutenant Commander Ewen Montagu; #find-charles, for research into Flight Lieutenant Charles Cholmondeley; #find-jean, for research into MI5 secretary Jean Leslie; and #find-bevan, for research into Colonel John Bevan. These individuals never needed to be 'found' the same way Hester did, with plenty already written about them. In the case of Montagu, he himself had authored two books that discussed Operation Mincemeat. Still, there was something intriguing behind the idea of digging through records and looking for these names, and perhaps finding something as yet uncovered. Records are continually being made available as organisations list them in online catalogues. While we knew a substantial amount more about any of them than we did about Hester, there was still the desire to look for new information, and the potential to find it.

As the Discord server grew, new people found their way

to the research channels and a few more had to be added. #find-haselden focused on Francis Haselden, who worked for the British Consulate in Spain, where the body was left. #find-willie was set up to research William Watkins, an American pilot who crashed in Spain just days before the deployment of the body and ended up attending the autopsy. The latter channel was needed after U.S. fans of the show began to have questions about the American character, and thought it might be worth pursuing a research project on him akin to the one conducted into Hester.

Each channel would become filled with new discoveries, links and images. Sometimes we were collating research that was already well-known, but often new pieces of information were being unearthed from primary sources and strung together in a way that no one had yet done. When something worked particularly well to further the Hester research project, we tried the same tactic for our other research subjects.

There was still no formal organisation and no leader. Anyone could join and, if they wanted to, anyone could depart, having decided they'd given as much time or expertise as they had to spare. People were active about spotting areas they had knowledge in and pursuing the necessary research in those spaces. Enquiries were sent by the people who were most likely to receive a reply based on the credentials in their email signatures, and visits to record-holding institutions were organised by those who could most easily make the journeys.

The first few months of the #FindingHester project saw great enthusiasm within the research team, but also a huge rise in numbers of those more generally considering themselves Mincefluencers. The show was gaining more attention, with impressive reviews in major publications and a cast album being listened to across the world. The days of playing to an 80-person audience at a fringe venue were long in the past and *Operation Mincemeat* was going from strength to strength. As the fan community grew, the virtual community on the Discord server similarly saw a fast growth in numbers. There was huge support for the #FindingHester project.

It got to the point where it was rather difficult for someone completely new to what we were doing to join in, as we'd woven ourselves a complicated web of research, and almost invariably any new suggestion of somewhere to look was either something we'd already explored and written off, or someone we'd already approached and were waiting to hear back from.

Some newer fans did lend useful expertise and knowledge, but for the most part, the membership of the #FindingHester team had been set, not because we were closed to new members but because anyone seeking to join had thousands of previous messages in the #find-hester channel to catch up on before they knew exactly what we were up to, and that was an understandably daunting task.

Regardless of their involvement in the research itself, the Mincefluencer community at large had a huge interest in the project. No one wanted to think that we'd been mis-remembering a woman by spelling her name wrong, but if that was truly the case then we all wanted to see it righted. The musical's version of Hester might not have minded, but there was a sense of justice-seeking that settled over the group.

ADDITIONAL RESEARCH: FINDING CHARLES

ERIN EDWARDS

THOROUGHLY bitten by the research bug, we weren't content to stop at researching Hester. With dedicated channels set up in the Discord server for the other individuals involved in the operation, a series of research tangents sprang up. One of those who we started with was Flight Lieutenant Charles Cholmondeley, an intelligence officer who helped dream up and enact the deception.

SpitLip's Cholmondeley is interpreted by many to be neurodivergent, bumbling his way through social situations and taking special interest in newts, maggots, and animals in general. He is the one who comes up with the plan for the operation, although he needs a bit of a push to advocate for his own ideas. In the finale number, dubbed the 'Glitzy Finale', where the characters outline their fates after the war, Charles explains that he isn't authorised to reveal what he got up to. He emphasises the need for discretion, the importance of doing one's duty and how it doesn't matter whether anyone knows as long as the good work is done.

The real Charles Cholmondeley's role in Operation Mincemeat is rather well documented, both in Ewen Montagu's books and in more contemporary research. Montagu even wrote a letter to *The Times* to serve as an obituary for him when he passed away in 1982. Cholmondeley never boasted about his experiences working at MI5, indeed he rarely seemed to mention it, and Montagu pointed out how many people owed their lives to him without ever even knowing his name, or what he did. Regardless, Cholmondeley's efforts made it into the history books eventually.

Details of his childhood discovery of a new type of shrew, his poor eyesight and his tall frame all survive, and all make it into SpitLip's portrayal, although early verses about the shrew discovery were later changed to a trout discovery. This is a reference to the Trout Memo, a document issued in 1939 by Admiral John Godfrey listing 54 ways the enemy could be fooled, as a trout is fooled by a lure. One of these suggestions would go on, developed by Montagu and Cholmondeley, to become Operation Mincemeat.

There is a good chance Cholmondeley might not have

been thrilled with the existence of a musical that shouts about his role in the war effort, nor about the film or the books or the podcasts. When *The Man Who Never Was Man Who Never Was*, a film based on Montagu's book by the same name, was made in 1956, Cholmondeley was referred to as George Acres. Presumably this was owing to his own request not to be identifiably included.

Cholmondeley went on to live a quiet life with his wife and children. His grave is engraved very simply with 'C.C.C.', with no dates of existence, no full name, and no reference to the exceptional work he did during the war. Just as he would have wanted.

With a fair amount of information about Cholmondeley already recorded, it was clear that any further research was going to have to be on a granular level, and likely prior to his role in the war. We started researching Hester by doing standard searches on family history websites, so we started there with Cholmondeley too.

Like Hester, Cholmondeley's life began outside of England, despite having an English family. He was born in Australia to a fairly large, vineyard-owning family who, following in the same tradition as the Leggatts, saw high value in education at an English public school. Cholmondley's father was Eton educated and none of his six children were educated in Australia. Cholmondeley was the youngest, with two older brothers and three older sisters. His father died the year after he was born.

When he attended school in England, his home address was recorded as Leighton Hall, Welshpool, residing with sisters Lettice and Victoria Millicent. Victoria was in her late twenties when her youngest brother started at school and was likely functioning as his guardian at the time.

Cholmondeley seems to have stayed close to his siblings throughout his life. From at least as early as 1941, he resided at Queen's Gate Place Mews in London with sister Victoria Millicent and mother Hilda Georgina, who was known by her second name. This would have been where he lived during the planning and carrying out of Operation Mincemeat, not far from Ewen Montagu and about an hour long walk to the MI5 London offices.

No bomb damage is recorded to the residence for the duration of the war, although one end of the road and several surrounding streets were less fortunate. It was luck more than anything else that saw the property remain intact. The three remained living there together until his mother moved away to Dorset and Cholmondeley married his wife. He would go on to have three children and, when he passed away in 1982, the notice of his death in *The Daily Telegraph* requested for donations to be made to Wells Day Centre or the British Schools Exploring Society, the latter reflecting a lifelong love of the outdoors.

When it came to further research into Cholmondeley, there were some school archivists in our group who were clued in to the wealth of information that often resides in these kinds of archives. He attended Canford School, a fairly young public school founded in 1923 but a public school nonetheless, which had us optimistic that they would have decent surviving records.

Cholmondeley turned up at the school in October 1930, aged 13, only seven years after it was founded. He was placed in Court House, where he would have boarded. In the usual tradition, a photograph was taken of the boys in the house every year and the Canford School archive contains digitised copies of each of these images, although they unfortunately lack captions that contain names. Today the most prevalent image of an older Cholmondeley is him in his military uniform, with his hair slicked back, his moustache neatly combed, and round tortoiseshell glasses to correct the poor eyesight that made him unsuitable for pilot training. Comparing this to the Court House images, there was only one boy in the photographs that could be Cholmondeley. His low brow, long neck and tall stature is visible in each image as he slowly gets older.

Another easily identifiable Cholmondeley appears in the 1934 Court House Rugby team photograph. In addition to House rugby, he also gained both House Colours and School Colours for shooting in 1935, recognising his success in the sport. SpitLip's musical presents a fairly uncoordinated Cholmondeley, with all the hallmarks of the nerd archetype, but despite appearing to be a rather gangly teenager, he was engaged in school sports in a way promoted by most public schools. This is not to suggest he was without academic success at school, however, as he won the third form mathematics prize at the end of his first year. He was also appointed a House Prefect in May 1935, holding the position until he left Canford at the end of that year.

Alongside the group sporting photographs, it is also possible he appears in some of the archive's 1933 O.T.C. photographs, although it is impossible to pick him out from the sea of uniformed pupils.

The Officers' Training Corps was formed of military units controlled by the British Army. Originally conceived in 1906 as a solution to the shortage of officers, the units were established at public schools for a junior division, and universities as a senior division. Boys were trained in military discipline, military tactics, and practical techniques. During World War One, over 20,000 officers were recruited from O.T.C. units. After the war, public school boys, including Cholmondeley, continued to train. He reached the rank of Lance-Corporal in February 1935 and passed the A Examination three months later.

It was an unremarkable O.T.C. experience when considering the role Cholmondeley would later play in World War Two. Ironically, it did consist of a higher than average amount of theoretical work, considering his military career would go on to consist of no active service. The weather in 1935 drove many of the practical training sessions for the Canford O.T.C. platoon inside, replacing them with lectures. It was probably exactly the kind of foundation Cholmondeley needed.

His O.T.C. career might have been underwhelming, but Cholmondeley's time in the First Canford Scout Troop went slightly differently. His first year at the school coincided with the first year it trialled a troop, with the enthusiasm of the students ensuring its continued operation. Although some boys couldn't adjust to the increased personal responsibility of moving from a preparatory school troop to a public school one, Cholmondeley was one of 18 boys who were committed to the activity.

Six of these boys embarked upon the first Canford Scout camp. With numbers so low, there was no point in campers staying in their usual patrols and instead one temporary patrol was formed, with Cholmondeley taking charge of the group despite being one of the younger boys at the school. Part of the camp experience involved a visit to the Gunnery School of the Royal Tank Corps, where the scouts were able to watch battle practice, view the workshops, and go for a ride on a tank. Even scouting, which was often seen as an alternative to the O.T.C., was not free from the militaristic influences that pervaded in a country with such recent memories of one war and increasing fears they would be facing another.

The First Canford Scout Troop grew throughout Cholmondeley's time at the school, gaining a scout hut and splitting the older boys into their own senior patrol. It's unclear whether he remained in the group for the entire duration of his school career, as the scout report in *The Canfordian*, the school's magazine, rarely mentions specific boys by name. He did certainly have a sustained interest in nature, however, serving as secretary for the school's Geological Society in 1934 and 1935, even if it's possible he left the scouts to join the O.T.C. *The Canfordian* does present scouting as an alternative that might be chosen for health or personal reasons, so it may not have been possible to do both.

Cholmondeley left Canford in November 1935 at the age of 18, although he would return as an Old Canfordian in March 1938, to lecture on his travels in Canada. His sister Victoria had travelled there 10 years earlier, perhaps inspiring him to take his own trip.

In his valete entry in *The Canfordian*, Cholmondeley is recorded as proceeding to Peterhouse College, Cambridge. The reasons for this are unclear, since this isn't where he ended up. Either it's an error in recordkeeping or he changed his mind, as he would actually go on to study geography at Keble College, Oxford.

Keble College's archives have not been digitised and made available online the way much of Canford's have, but we were able to reach out to the college archivist to make specific enquiries about Cholmondeley. He joined the college on the 9th October 1936, then 19 years old.

In the early 1930s there was a great deal of enthusiasm for rugby at Keble, which might have suited Cholmonde-ley well, owing to his time playing for the Court House rugby team at Canford, but by the end of the decade, the popularity of the sport was waning. Hockey, whose players had once complained about rugby taking all the best sportsmen, drew Cholmondeley's attention instead, and he played in the college hockey team from 1937 to 1939. He is pictured in two team photos from this time, midway between the boy in his school photos and the man pictured in his Air Force uniform.

The University of Oxford had its own numbering system for its degrees at this time, and would do so until the 1970s. Their four divisions were numbered first, second, third and fourth class, as opposed to the typical tradition of first, upper second, lower second and third. Cholmondeley sat an agriculture prelim in 1937, but it was his 1939 examination that dictated the outcome of his time at Oxford: a fourth class geography degree.

As World War Two was already underway and large numbers of university students were either leaving courses early to enlist, or enlisting immediately after finishing the course, baccalaureates were not awarded during the course of the war. Graduation ceremonies would have been particularly sparsely attended. In 1945, once the war had come to an end, ceremonies were held for those who had completed their degrees in the last six years. Charles

Cholmondeley did not attend. One can only assume that the MBE he had been awarded in 1944 rather outranked a fourth class geography degree, even if it was from Oxford.

Cholmondeley is not Keble's only link to MI5 during World War Two. In what appears to be a complete coincidence, MI5 co-opted the college to use as residential space. Many members of the Security Service had been moved to Wormwood Scrubs, a West London prison, once the lack of space in Central London had become an increasing problem. The building then saw significant damage during the Blitz, and the majority of the staff were relocated to Blenheim Palace, near Oxford.

It is presumably at this point that Keble was being used by MI5, avoiding overlapping with Cholmondeley's time there by only about a year and a half. During his time at MI5 working on Operation Mincemeat, he was working in London in camouflaged offices on St James's Street. In the meantime, papers in the National Archive reveal that Keble was being used to house 250 members of MI5's female staff, and had a 'complete Civil Defence and Fire Fighting Organisation'. Hester was not amongst this number of 250, instead working on St James's Street alongside Cholmondeley.

After World War Two, Charles Cholmondeley took up a job as a First Locust Officer with the Middle East Anti-Locust Unit. This may seem like a strange career change, but in many other ways it is in line with much of the rest of what we know about him. Between this job and his shrew discovery earlier in life, SpitLip made their version of Cholmondeley particularly interested in all kinds of animals. He's teased at the office for being a 'bug boy', although he prefers the term 'amateur naturalist'. There's a recurring joke about his knowledge of newts, and his solo song, *Dead in the Water* has him comparing himself to a laundry list of animals that all seem better suited to their environments than he feels he is suited to the environment of MI5.

Cholmondeley appears in a series of National Archive files regarding his work as First Locust Officer, signing documents with a rather messy 'Charles' that is hard to make out unless you know what you're looking at. One of such signatures is attached to a report on the 1948 activities of the 'Qasim Detachment', of which Cholmondeley was a part. In it, one of the men Cholmondeley was travelling with on route to Kuwait was involved in a jeep accident, with the vehicle overturning and crushing his thigh, resulting in a trip via ambulance to a hospital in Kuwait. The announcement that he 'was in hospital there within 24 hours of the accident occurring' is worded as an achievement, and it probably was, given the remote location, but Lee-Oldfield, the injured man, likely didn't think so at the time.

The report goes on to detail Cholmondeley's movements across the Middle East: from Kuwait to Qasim to Jeddah, to Mahad, to Aglat. Although some place names have changed, this put Cholmondeley in the region of Saudi Arabia and Iraq. Once the Second Locust Officer, Hewitt, took over from Cholmondeley, he was free to hand over control of the detachment and conduct reconnaissance for three weeks. Strictly into locusts, of course.

There were pages of the report cataloguing locust swarms, documenting their location, behaviour, size and colour, as well as keeping an eye on hatching rates. After details of the locusts, however, the reports cover the political developments in the region, detailing any changes amongst those in power. This alone might not be enough to conclusively prove that Cholmondeley was perhaps looking for more than just locusts but, considering he would go on to work with MI5 again, only leaving in 1952, it does seem very likely that he was engaged in work for the Secret Service while in the Middle East. If SpitLip are ever looking to write a sequel musical to *Operation Mincemeat*, the perfect source material is ready and waiting.

CHAPTER FOUR

MAKING A HERO

IT didn't take long to establish the broad strokes of Hester's life, but we wanted to find everything of her that was out there. It felt important to return an identity to her that was grounded in something other than just her marital status, which had dominated her memory so much.

With a fair level of confidence in the correct spelling of Hester's surname, we began to put it, along with her dates of birth and death, into different databases. There was the potential for her to be mentioned anywhere, with no one else using the correct name to look for her before. Searching online newspaper archives gave us some early successes.

In 1917, an 11-year-old Hester took the Royal Academy of Music and Royal College of Music Primary Division pianoforte examination under the tutelage of Miss Burnside Clayton. Her success was listed in the West Surrey Times on 19th January. She continued to practice the instrument and went on to pass the Elementary

Division of the same examinations the following year. In the second article, from 4th May 1918, Hester's school is identified as Tormead School, Guildford.

The discovery that Hester played piano was, on the surface, fairly mundane, but it represented one of the first things we learnt about her that went beyond census data. It was a little piece of individuality. It was also one of the first of many coincidental but enjoyable links to the musical. In Hester's solo *Dear Bill*, she describes spending time with the family of her soldier while he's deployed, leaving it ambiguous whether this is a fictitious situation invented for 'Pam' during World War Two, or whether she is drawing on her own experience in World War One. Perhaps it's both.

In the letter she's crafting, she informs the soldier that his younger sister has been enthusiastically practicing piano so she can play perfectly when he gets home. She continually plays *We Wish You a Merry Christmas* despite it still being summer, preparing for his return for the festive season in an acknowledgement of that popular phrase in 1914: 'the war will be over by Christmas'.

To so quickly and rather easily find this evidence of the real Hester learning piano felt serendipitous, with the musical's cast equally surprised but thrilled by the revelation. It was almost like they'd planned it, and if you ask them, they might try to convince you they did, but there was no way they could have done.

The piano examinations also provided the name of the school Hester had attended prior to Wycombe Abbey, as we'd already discovered in the census. Tormead School was the same age as Hester, founded in 1905 by Countess Zola Waloska in Guildford. It began in a house on Lower Edgebrook Road, ready to teach the daughters of parents hoping to give their girls an education, perhaps even with the goal of employment in mind. With two older brothers in private education already, it may have seemed only sensible to Hester's parents to treat her in a similar way, particularly if they wanted her to grow up in England.

By the time Hester attended the school, it had moved to its current site at Tormead House, which provided its name, a portmanteau of 'Torquay', where the family who owned the house was initially from, and 'meadow', for the one the house stood in. From the newspaper articles, she attended in 1917 and 1918, but may well have started younger.

Our attempts to learn much more about her time there have been unsuccessful, but it seems it was more of a preparatory school for her than anything else, as we already knew she moved on to Wycombe Abbey, even though she could have continued her education at Tormead.

The discovery of Hester's school in the 1921 census had provided an excellent lead for a potential source of information. Wycombe Abbey is a private school for girls located in High Wycombe. Established in 1896, it boasts actresses, authors, suffragettes, MPs and journalists amongst its alumnae. Dame Frances founded her school with the belief that girls deserved equal education and ought to be taught corporate virtues and discipline and have a wide set of interests. By the time of Hester's arrival at the school, Miss Whitelaw had taken over as Head Mistress, but Dame Frances' values still seem to have been lauded, as would be shown by Hester's busy school life.

Wycombe Abbey had no knowledge of Hester when we first reached out. Like all private schools, they keep track of their notable alumnae, both alive and deceased, but there was no known link to MI5 or Operation Mincemeat that had been passed back to the school. They operate what are known as Circles, where their Seniors (the term for Wycombe Abbey alumnae) keep in touch via a nominated Circle Secretary who passes on news from the school and collects news from the Circle to report back. Hester never shared the extent of her activities in the War Office, valuing the secrecy of her work until her death.

There was no official archivist employed at Wycombe Abbey when we reached out, so it was the Alumnae Relations Officer who answered the email. Thankfully, the lack of archivist didn't mean the lack of archival records, and she was able to use a school roll to confirm Hester's enrolment. Hester entered Wycombe Abbey on 5th May 1920, one year before the census places her there, and left in July 1924. While at the school she resided in Barry House.

Thankfully, the school was enthusiastic to learn about our research into Hester and was kind enough to go through the issues of their magazine, *The Gazette*, that covered her time there. She is mentioned in the list of new girls in May 1920 and again in December 1922, when she gained her School Certificate. To do so required the grade of at least a pass, if not a credit or distinction, in six subjects, including English and mathematics.

In the 1922 issue of the magazine Hester is also listed as the 'House Editor' for Barry House, a job of which no one is quite sure of the meaning. It completes a trio of roles after House Head and House Captain, and is also mirrored at a school-wide level, with a 'School Editor' named on the same page. A logical inference suggests possibly a position of responsibility when it came to *The Gazette* or involvement with recordkeeping within the house. Whatever it was, perhaps it would go on to serve her well in providing a basis for her keen secretarial eye.

Hester's archival footprint at Wycombe Abbey follows the expected path. She was Confirmed in December 1921 in a group of 39 girls at a service led by the Bishop of Oxford. In June 1923, she passed the London General Schools Examination with exemption from London Matriculation, which would have allowed her to enter the University of London without taking a further matriculation examination.

A successful academic record is not Hester's only Wycombe Abbey achievement. She also appears to have been part of the school's guiding group. Just as Wycombe Abbey was begun by a woman who believed girls deserved the same education as boys, the Guide Association was founded in 1909, in order to give girls the same opportunities boys were receiving through scouting.

Still a foundational childhood activity for young girls across the country today, guiding would have seen Hester working towards a range of badges to prove she'd mastered what were seen as core life skills. The Clerk badge, requiring the ability to use a typewriter, might have been of interest to her, but other early guiding badges included the Cook badge, for which one had to be able to skin and clean a rabbit; the Flyer badge, which could be achieved through having a certificate for flying a plane; the Rifleshot badge, which specified a minimum accuracy; or the Telegraphist badge, which required elementary understanding of electricity and the ability to read and send Morse code.

Unfortunately, no record survives of exactly what badges Hester earned, but *The Gazette* does carry a report of 'an Entertainment' put on by the Guides at the school in March 1923. This began with games and folk dancing, followed by a series of depictions of the intervention of industrious Guides in historical catastrophes, featuring characters such as Joan of Arc and Boadicea.

Hester's role in the performance was to read a piece of writing by A.A. Milne. Famous most substantially for *Winnie the Pooh*, Milne was rather prolific and penned a number of works aimed most often at children. In a mostly forgotten book of short stories entitled *Happy Days*, he published a story entitled 'A Simple English Girl', number 98 in the collection. The plot follows 18-year-old Gwendolen French, the daughter of a farmer, and her chance encounter with Lord Beltravers of Beltravers Castle, upon his return from India.

Falling in love with Gwendolen on sight owing to her beauty, Lord Beltravers invites her to a ball at the castle, where he asks her to marry him. She accepts, but Lord Beltravers' mother is horrified by the idea of her son marrying a commoner. She travels to the farm to request Gwendolen's father reason with his daughter, but finds instead a man who she herself had once turned down a proposal from. Once Earl of Turbot, he had chosen a simple life as a farmer after being refused, but his identity as an Earl means his daughter is actually Lady Gwendolen Hake, who is a perfectly acceptable match for Lord Beltravers. It ends, as these stories tend to do, with a wedding and a happily ever after.

It is the first chapter, entitled 'Primrose Farm', of this story that Hester read at Wycombe Abbey. It is coincidence alone that it contains a case of forgotten and subsequently rediscovered identity, but a satisfying coincidence, nonetheless. As she read, the scenes were acted out in mime by the Scarlet Pimpernel Patrol. The narration was followed by a campfire scene and the singing of the national anthem, with the entire event considered a great success.

Hester was starting to take shape. With every new piece of information, we were able to add to a picture of her that felt very human. The more we learnt, the more there was to feel a connection to. We'd all experienced the various parts of school life that Hester had and it became easier to see her as a person, as a student or a sister or a daughter, rather than a bitter spinster. And with every new thing we learnt, we were reminded that there had to be more out there that could expand the Hester we were slowly uncovering.

It was going to be easiest to trace Hester throughout her life if we could work chronologically, with each stage ideally leading neatly into the next, so we specifically requested any information the school might hold on what she went on to do once she left. Girls have been receiving univer-sity education in the UK since 1868, when nine women were enrolled at the University of London, although the first woman to gain honours equal to a man would not be awarded her degree until 1920, for exams she actually passed in 1877. It was not impossible that Hester could have gone on to university, but it also would not have been the standard progression for girls at the time.

Thankfully the staff at Wycombe Abbey were willing to

do some further digging on our behalf. The school kept Senior Roll books in which seniors recorded their details of their time there. In Hester's own handwriting, we can see that she left at the end of the second term in 1924, after '4 1/3' years. She lists her predominant accomplishments during her time at the school as 'House monitor, House Editor, Library Committee. Qualified for plain needlework, London matric: June 1923. Position badge.' 'School board' is also added at the end in pencil.

At this point, we were unsure whether we'd found a sample of Hester's handwriting other than the 'Pam' letters. A trip to The National Archives had revealed a September 1949 Certificate of Registration as Citizen of the United Kingdom and Colonies. Following the British Nationality Act 1948. Hester, born in India, had to register as a British citizen owing to the British Empire becoming the Commonwealth. Prior to this, everyone in the Empire was a 'British subject'. This form contained Hester's name, address, father's name, details of her birth, and the reason she believed she could claim to be a British subject without citizenship: 'I was born in India'.

When looking at this form, it was unclear whether we could match it to the writing on the 'Pam' letters. The letters were purposefully written to seem girlish and rushed, in a way that might have meant Hester adapted her usual handwriting for them, so comparing them to samples from more natural writing was more difficult.

There was also some question of whether the citizenship form had been filled in by Hester or on her behalf by an administrative assistant, but the personal identification of 'I was born in India' seemed to imply this was Hester herself. With the addition of the handwriting sample provided by Wycombe Abbey from the Senior Roll book, we were able to get a better sense of Hester's handwriting and the similarities and differences across samples, and were able to conclude that the citizenship form, the Senior Roll entry, and the 'Pam' letters were almost certainly all written by the same person.

The most important document for our continuing research that Wycombe Abbey provided, however, was her war record. In a volume comprising of short entries to keep up with their alumnae during World War Two, Hester's entry specified that she proceeded from Wycombe Abbey to St James' Secretarial College, London. A line below that reads 'Ministry. War Office, London.'

This was the closest we had gotten to definitive confirmation linking the Hester we'd been researching to the Hester who worked on Operation Mincemeat. There was no further clarification of exactly what she had been doing in the War Office, but the record was likely penned prior to 1945, based on the included address of '13 Beaufort Gardens, SW3', which is where she resides in the 1945 electoral roll. By the 1946 electoral roll, she had moved to 102 Queen's Gate.

The Official Secrets Act, which made it a criminal offence for employees of the State to disclose any official information, kept many people from talking about their work during the war. Some went their entire lives without divulging the details of how they served their country, with Hester herself seemingly amongst the number that opted to keep their secrets. 'War Office' was certainly as precise as she could have gotten in 1945, but it lacked the specificity many of us craved. Still, it was a reassuring sight, and it would be a little while longer before we had anything more concrete to undeniably establish the link between Hester May Murray Leggatt and Operation Mincemeat.

In the meantime, we turned to St James's Secretarial College, hoping we might be able to use their records to follow Hester through her post-school life. It had been a highly-regarded finishing school, founded in 1912 by Monica Spencer-Munt, who had been private secretary to Lord Churchill, and boasting one of the top secretarial courses in the country.

After the involvement of women in war work during World War One, young women were increasingly interested in forming their own careers, at least until they married. Secretarial courses became a popular path into a respectable profession, teaching not just secretarial skills but presentation and decorum.

Reaching out to Wycombe Abbey had been such a

successful process that we had high hopes when we went looking for records at St James's Secretarial College. It no longer exists as its own organisation, merging with Queen's Secretarial College and the Lucie Clayton Charm Academy in 2007. There is now much less of a demand for specific secretarial training, and finishing schools have long fallen out of fashion, so the merger saw a rebrand as Quest Business Training, now known as Quest Professional, and sees students learning IT skills, leadership and management, and sales and marketing.

As soon as we learnt about the merging of the schools, we already knew our chances of surviving records were slim. Sure enough, Quest Professional keeps no records on the three organisations that form its history and are unsure where these records would have gone if they survived until 2007.

Our hopes of following one easy, unbroken line through Hester's working life had already been dashed, but we had far too much momentum to simply give up.

Our searches through online newspaper archives had also revealed Hester's attendance at the wedding of Esme Langton and Geoffrey George Fenner Greig in July 1928. News coverage of the event is particularly fulsome, noting that it was the first marriage solemnised at the New Charterhouse Chapel, while Esme's parents had been the first couple to marry in the Old Charterhouse Chapel. Hester was close enough to the bride to be one of five bridesmaids, but it is unclear exactly how they knew each other. Esme's father was a housemaster of Gownboys boarding house at Charterhouse during the period that Hester's brother Donald was a pupil there, providing one theory.

Hester's whereabouts from 1911 to 1917 is unclear, so it is feasible she could have been in England with her brother at this time. With the two girls almost the same age, it's easy to imagine romanticised pastoral scenes of them running around the grounds of Charterhouse together as pre-teens. While we can't say that did happen, and it does seem a little farfetched, there is a fair chance that they first met around this time. Esme attended neither Tormead School nor Wycombe Abbey and, as far as we can tell in the absence of surviving records, she also did not attend St James's Secretarial College, so she and Hester must have met socially one way or another.

Esme and Geoffrey's wedding is lavishly described in the *Daily Mirror*, the *Surrey Advisor* and the *West Sussex Gazette*, on what one can only assume was an otherwise slow news day. After a procession from Gownboys boarding house and along the terrace in front of the main Charterhouse buildings, the ceremony was performed by the Bishop of Guildford. The reception was held at The Hall at Charterhouse and attended by 400 guests, with the papers reporting the couple received 300 gifts. 100 guests presumably added their name to a gift their significant other had chosen, in a scene familiar to all wedding attendees today. Following the day, the newlyweds left for a honeymoon motoring around North Wales.

But why did we care so much about Esme and Geoffrey? It's not like it was Hester's wedding.

We had begun this journey knowing nothing about Hester Leggatt, not even the correct spelling of her name, and now we knew exactly how she had spent her day on 24th July 1928. We knew where she'd walked in the procession to the chapel, we knew she'd sung the hymns *The King of Love*, *Lift up your hearts*, and *Now thank we all our God*. Perhaps she'd smelt the orange blossoms in Esme's coronet, or the flame-coloured gladioli that she was carrying as one of the bridesmaids. She must have thanked Geoffrey for his gift of a choker necklace that he provided to all the women in the wedding party. Maybe she complimented her friend on her wedding dress, a duchess satin frock with a gold lamé train embroidered with lily of the valley and embellished with pearls.

Hester herself would have been in a dress of green floral ninon, with a scalloped hem in three shades of green, a long scarf, and a coronet of green leaves. We put the questionable sounding outfit choice down to the time period, rather than any hidden spite on Esme's part. The 1920s was a fairly experimental time for fashion.

All of these details from the newspaper articles covering the wedding are often minute, arguably mundane, and answer questions we would never have thought to ask in a lifetime of research. We might have gladly traded them in at the time for answers to some of our more pressing, fundamental questions about Hester's career, but there is still a huge amount of value in them. They allow us to visualise an entire day in the life of Hester Leggatt, a level of intimacy that we had not dreamt of when initially faced with just an incorrect name and vague dates of existence. This was a day Hester spent in celebration of her friend, sandwiched between two world wars, and very possibly cursing a terribly ugly bridesmaid dress she'd been made to wear. It holds a great deal of sentiment and humanity.

ADDITIONAL RESEARCH: FINDING EWEN

ERIN EDWARDS

IF there is anyone associated with Operation Mincemeat who never needed to be found, it is Ewen Montagu. He's the centre of every major retelling of the story, mostly because he wrote the original book about it.

After the end of World War Two, Ewen Montagu fought persistently for the right to tell the story of Operation Mincemeat. The publication of Alfred Duff Cooper's *Operation Heartbreak* in 1950 made him even more determined. Once this fictionalised version of events was out there, there was nothing to be gained in keeping the secrets of the real operation.

Three years later, Montagu had worn the necessary people down and was permitted to publish a slightly censored version of the tale in *The Man Who Never Was*

Man Who Never Was. Cholmondeley wasn't named, likely by his own request, and the identity of the corpse as Welshman Glyndwr Michael wasn't revealed until 1996, but Montagu's book laid out the real story of Operation Mincemeat for the public for the first time. In 1956, it was made into a BAFTA-winning film of the same name. While Montagu's character was played by American actor Clifton Webb, Montagu himself had a cameo in the film as an Air Vice Marshal who raises doubts about the feasibility of the plan.

Still, Montagu wasn't quite satisfied that he'd told the story the way he wanted. In 1977 he published *Beyond Top Secret U*, a book that looks more widely into his role in Naval Intelligence and returns to the Operation Mincemeat story to fill in some gaps that he could now discuss.

With all of this first-hand information, Lieutenant Commander Ewen Montagu CBE QC DL was never lost.

He was born in 1901 to Jewish parents, and died in 1985, three years after Charles Cholmondeley. Montagu was the middle son of three, with one sister younger than all of them, and the entire family lived a fairly privileged life. He attended Westminster School with both his brothers and was just too young to ever see active service in World War One. Perhaps this was why he enlisted in the Royal Navy Volunteer Reserve in 1938, with another world war about to play out.

By this time, Montagu had studied at Trinity College

Cambridge and at Harvard. He pursued a legal career and was doing rather a good job of it before this new wave of conflict arrived.

Montagu owned a yacht and was at home on the water, but he was denied the chance to serve at sea. Considering his legal background, he was reassigned to intelligence work, working on the Double Cross system that managed the double agents MI5 were puppeteering during the War.

Considering his work at the heart of British Intelligence and his Jewish identity, Montagu feared for the fate of his wife and two children if Germany were to invade Britain. To keep them safe, he sent them to America for several years and saw very little of them until they returned to England in September 1943. In the meantime, he moved back into his family home and slept in the basement, owing to its increased protection in the event of an air raid.

When Montagu's wife and two young children returned to England, the Blitz was over but the V1 and V2 bombs would still cause significant devastation. Montagu knew these weapons were being developed but was unable to share with his family just how dangerous London might still be once they returned. He kept the information confidential, as was his job, but keeping it from his wife was something he remembered as particularly difficult. Thankfully, the family was unharmed.

After the war, Montagu returned to his legal work,

holding the position of Judge Advocate of the Fleet from 1945 to 1973, which had him supervising the Royal Navy's Court Martial system. He also relentlessly wrote letters to the higher-ups keeping Operation Mincemeat's secrets under wraps until long after the war, desperate for his chance to tell the story. It clearly never left his mind, if his obituary for Cholmondeley is anything to go by.

With all that already known, we never had to do the same detective work as we did with Hester to ascertain whether we were even dealing with the right person, but that didn't mean there was nothing out there to find. With the childhood research into Hester and Cholmondeley proving so fruitful, we turned to a pre-Operation Mincemeat Montagu, hoping to look at records which had gone unexplored in previous considerations of him.

Ewen Montagu attended Westminster School, a public school across the road from the Houses of Parliament. He joined at the same time as his older brother, Stuart Albert Montagu, who was heir to the family title. Their younger brother, Ivor Montagu, would join them in 1917. All three joined boarding houses but were considered half-boarders, returning home on the weekends owing to their Jewish faith, so they could observe their religion at home and avoid mandatory Sunday morning services in Westminster Abbey.

Westminster School's archive has been extensively catalogued in the last decade or so, and we had access to every potential document he could have appeared in: magazines, ledgers, and photographs. We began with the Record of Old Westminsters, a catalogue of all known school alumni. Each entry covers not only a boy's time at the school, but also their careers once they left. These additional details were usually self-reported in answers to questionnaires sent to Old Westminsters. Montagu's entry is fairly comprehensive, and most of the information was nothing new to us but, significant for our research, it contained details of his time at the school: his admission and leaving dates, 1914-1919, and his house, Rigaud's.

Rigaud's is the second oldest boarding house at Westminster School, after Grant's, the oldest continuous public school boarding house, if not counting College, which boards the school's scholars. It is based in the right-hand side of what was once a mirrored terrace of three almost identical residences. The portion that made up Rigaud's was knocked down and rebuilt prior to Montagu's admittance, leaving it an orange brick building, out of place compared to the two black brick frontages to its left. Both of Montagu's brothers boarded next door in Grant's but, whether by choice or through lack of space, he did not.

Knowing Montagu's house, we turned to the archives collection of Rigaud's house photographs in the hope of unearthing an image of him as a teenager. Unfortunately, the series has some gaps near the start of the 20th century, including one which perfectly eclipses Montagu's time at the school.

What does survive in the collection, however, is a whole school photograph from 1919. In 1976, a key of this photograph was created by Richard Seymour Chalk, an Old Westminster who attended the school from 1918-1924 and was gifted with a remarkable memory. Even though his time at the school overlapped with Montagu's only briefly, Chalk does correctly name him, but even without this key, it would have been an obvious identification. Aged 18, Montagu already very closely resembled the man in the photographs associated with Operation Mincemeat.

Hoping for more luck in the written records than with the photographs, we turned to the school's collection of Rigaud's house documents, finding that Montagu's name appeared several times. In Lent Term 1916, he is noted as having come down with 'German measles', now usually known as Rubella, amid a house-wide epidemic. Illness spread quickly throughout boarding schools, so it was not uncommon for a house, or the entire school, to be shut down for a short period of time in order to stop the spread of infection.

A decade and a half before Charles Cholmondeley was involved in the O.T.C., Ewen Montagu also participated. For him, the existence of active warfare with no end in sight likely meant that he spent his O.T.C. drills fully expecting to be sent to the front himself before the conflict came to an end. His older brother had left the school after only one year to serve with the Grenadier Guards. Montagu avoided the same experience by a timespan of only eight months.

Despite never seeing active combat in World War One, it still came knocking at his door. The school magazine frequently published lists of Old Westminsters known to be engaged in the war effort, as well as those who had lost their lives. Contemporary pupils recalled a Zeppelin raid in October 1915. Shots were heard at 9.25pm, followed by cries of 'the Zepps are here'. Most of the house was immediately sent down to the changing room to utilise it as a kind of shelter, but reportedly 'made enough noise in doing it to attract all the Zeppelins in Christendom.'

Lights were turned out on the order of a passing constable and the boys not taking shelter watched guns from St. James's Park, Charing Cross and Lambeth Bridge fire on a Zeppelin that looked close enough to be over the Abbey, but was in actuality a little further away, over the Lyceum Theatre on the Strand. The Zeppelin managed to drop a small number of bombs before it took off down the Thames.

Within half an hour, calm had returned. The older boys who had escaped the evacuation down to the changing room were thrilled to have had such a good view. It was recorded in the Rigaud's House ledger as a bit of fun, and for teenage boys seeking any excuse to be distracted from their work, it probably was. Many of the same boys would soon face the front lines themselves, where gunfire was no longer an exciting change of pace.

Air raids also pepper the school timetable, considered a 'blessing in disguise' for getting rid of early morning prep, when pupils were expected to be working. The Head Master would ring a bell, disrupting 'sleep or prep (same thing in some people's case)', and boys would grab rugs to stay warm, and books to entertain themselves while they waited out the raid in the changing room.

In December 1917 the raids were so frequent that the Head of Rigaud's, the boy in charge of keeping the ledger, admitted to not seeing the point of noting down all the dates. He instead concludes that 'suffice to say that they were greeted at the beginning of the term by cheers and at the end of the term by groans.'

This was Montagu's Westminster. The war was both immediate and ever-present, and endlessly far away.

Even with a brother off fighting and frequent air raids, school life went on as normal. In Election Term 1918, Montagu found himself on the house cricket team, and in 1919 he was on the house swimming team. Neither saw much success but it seems unfair to place the blame for that solely on Montagu's shoulders. In another similarity to Cholmondeley, and one to Hester, he was also made a monitor towards the end of his school career.

The chess ledger revealed that Montagu also spent a stint

as a member of the school's chess club. The club often struggled to maintain a steady membership and phased in and out of activity. In 1919 they opted to formalise membership as a group of 32 elected pupils. Montagu was chosen as one of them, but resigned from his place further down on the same page of the ledger. It was instead given to his younger brother, Ivor. Two rules were passed on the same occasion, one of which regarded how game disputes were to be handled. The other was as follows: 'That there shall be no eating during any Meeting of the Club'.

All common sense would suggest these were simply part of the re-establishment of the club, but one cannot help but wonder if Montagu resigned in protest at the outlawing of snacks at chess club meetings. He did go on to form a cheese-eating society at university, after all.

Proving himself rather a jack-of-all-trades, Montagu also took part in the Rigaud's Literary Society's reading of Shakespeare's *The Tempest*, allocated the part of Sebastian. The reading was judged entertaining, despite complaints that not enough life was put into parts, 'especially evident in the way in which they spoke of the deaths and subsequent revivals of their nearest relations in the same tone of voice in which they discussed the climate.'

Several boys were lambasted for poor pronunciation, but Montagu's Sebastian was hailed as something of a prophet when his decree that 'by and by it will strike' was heeded by the clock above the fire, which dutifully obliged.

Montagu also spent a three week stint at a Harvest Camp during his time at the school, travelling down to Brede in Sussex. The boys worked for seven and a half hours a day and on the final day had to cycle eight hours back to the train station through a thunderstorm, with the Head of House recalling 'we were wet before we started, we were soaked when we reached the station, then as a kind of last straw the roof of the railway carriage leaked.'

In behaviour perhaps not unexpected from a group of boys with minimal adult supervision, they had spent the final night of the camp fighting amongst each other at midnight. It is recalled as a 'cheerful scrap', but consisted of the Head of House succeeding in 'half killing Montagu' before they banded together to launch an attack on a nearby tent instead. Presumably Montagu arrived back at Westminster a little worse for wear, soaked through and bearing the evidence of the fight.

With Montagu's childhood a little more fleshed out, we posted one of his school photographs in the Discord and were met with a slightly puzzled response from one of the other server members. That was his great-grandfather in the picture, and he had never seen that photograph. Where had we got it from? After some explanation on both sides, we learnt we had a Ewen Montagu expert in our midst – by virtue of blood relation.

The Montagu family have been fans of the musical since

its early days, going to see it, unprompted by the creators, during its run at the New Diorama Theatre. Both of his children, his grandchildren, and his great-grandchildren have all seen it. One of the cast members does remember a family member having to explain to Montagu's son, Jeremy, during an early scene that his father was being played by a woman. But the family have embraced the production and given it their approval, believing it would have appealed to Montagu's sense of humour.

As well as the books Montagu published, he also wrote an unpublished autobiography for his family, which they were kind enough to share parts of with us. They were also incredibly generous in answering ridiculously specific questions we'd racked up during our early research. The announcement of Montagu's impending marriage to Iris Solomon was accompanied in the newspaper by an image of the two of them sitting together, with Montagu holding a terrier on his knees. Fully expecting to be told no one had any idea, we asked the name of the dog. Within minutes, we had an answer. That was Pip. One hundred years of distance never feels quite as insignificant as when you can put a name to a family pet in a photograph.

It is possible Pip might have been something of a terror. In Ivor Montagu's autobiography, he recalls a fair menagerie of animals at the Montagu family home throughout his childhood, most notable of which has to be his white angora rabbit, named Ferocity. He also mentions, however, the sad fate of a pet hedgehog which was killed by Ewen's dog. There is no mention of a name with the tale so we can't be certain it is the same dog, but it does seem likely that the innocent little face in the newspaper photograph was harbouring a history of hedgehog murder.

One of the most interesting mentions of Montagu in the Westminster School archive came from the school's magazine, *The Elizabethan*. Each house was given a House Notes section to record any announcements or updates. The December 1918 Rigaud's House Notes section recorded that 'We are glad to see that Montagu, who has recovered from a severe motor bicycle accident, [is] once more among us.'

Despite a trawl through both House documents and *The Elizabethan*, there was no record of this motorbike accident actually occurring, leaving us with plenty of questions. The vehicles weren't hugely popular in England at this time, with the largest UK motorbike producer manufacturing only 500 units a year in 1903. World War One saw their increased popularity by the forces, but public ownership and use still wasn't common. Letting a 17-year-old ride one was an interesting choice.

With a direct line to undoubtedly the world experts in Ewen Montagu, we couldn't resist asking if they knew the full story. It felt like a long shot, considering how much time had passed, but if Pip's name endured, maybe this did, too. To our delight, one of his granddaughters could provide the entire story, in full detail and with a tone that felt reminiscent of Montagu's own books.

Earlier in the war, Montagu had trained as an instructor at the National Guard Machine Gun School and was proficient in firing five types of machine gun. When he found out the American Naval Air Force were stationed at Eastleigh airport, he mentioned his qualifications and the American Commanding Officer, Commander Chevalier, was keen to bring him onboard to help teach the firing of Vickers and Lewis machine guns, which few of his men had experience with.

Montagu had been given a motorbike to facilitate his journey to the base. The route included a road with an S-bend that Montagu always took partially by travelling onto the wrong side of the road to straighten out the curve. In an age of minimal motor traffic, this was not quite as risky as it would be today, but on this occasion, he was unfortunate enough to encounter a car coming in the other direction who was also adopting the same technique of approaching the curve. Crashing into the bonnet, he flew over his handlebars. Montagu maintained that it was only down to luck that he didn't castrate himself in the process, as he had, by chance, removed the large speedometer between the handlebars only the day before in order to get the broken glass cover mended.

If you load up Google Maps and go looking for Eastleigh

railway station, you will find Bishopstoke's Road. It crosses the railway track and then curves around the station building in a noticeable 'S' shape. The site of the motorbike crash could be narrowed down to a 100-metre stretch of road. To go from an oblique reference in a school magazine to the full story, complete with commentary from Montagu himself, was incredibly exciting.

The pages of Montagu's unpublished memoir also reveal more about his time at school. He recalled his classics being poor, which saw him placed into the lowest form. Despite being adept at maths, the lower school's maths lessons posed no challenge to or even use of his skill and he lost much of it through misuse. His housemaster was remembered as 'appallingly bad', wily and cunning but too distant for any of the boys to get to know. Amongst his recollections of Rigaud's, Montagu notes the changing room in the basement, where he likely spent much time in the dark during air raids, as well as the presence of two baths to serve the entire house. Each boy had one cold bath a day and one hot bath a week.

Montagu cited an enjoyment of Eton Fives, a game similar to squash played by two teams of two boys. The small ball is hit with gloved hands and the three-sided court is a highly specific shape. The origins of the game saw it played against the exterior of the Eton School chapel and thus every Eton Fives court takes the same shape as this architecture, including a buttress, two levels separated by a six-inch step, and a series of ledges. Many of these quirks are used strategically in gameplay but even those which serve no purpose are maintained in all courts.

Despite having no real interest in the sport, Montagu did also once find himself playing racquets for Rigaud's in a house tournament by virtue of being the only person available who had played even once before. Paired up with the school's top player, he was carried through to the final but the pair wasn't quite able to take the victory.

Sports made up many of Montagu's memories from Westminster, from football to cricket. He never claimed to be much good at the former, but felt overlooked for the latter. The second best wicket-keeper in the school, he never made it to Westminster's First XI, but would play for the Town Boys (all boys who were not Scholars, regardless of house) in their matches against the King's Scholars.

It was through cricket that he earned his House Colours, as well as his Third XI school colours (pink and black). There were no Second XI matches so their colours, pink and white, were reserved for boys who never made the First XI but played for the school as a substitute. The good health of the school's top-class wicket-keeper was Montagu's bad luck and he never got to play on the school team for even a single match.

One of Montagu's other defining memories of school was the system of discipline. Once he was a monitor, he would have been in charge of maintaining it. Trials were held within each house on the occasion of rule-breaking and misbehaviour, and the results were recorded into a black book. This book unfortunately doesn't survive in the archives, but Montagu used his time as a monitor to take the opportunity to look back over his time at the school as told through punishments. He had received the highest number of tannings, or beatings, in one term during all the years of the book's operation.

Corporal punishment was very much legal at this time, only outlawed in state schools in 1986 and English public schools in 1998. It was often seen by boys as a gentlemanly way to be punished. Even when given the choice between writing lines and being tanned, boys would choose the latter, not wanting to be seen as weak for shying away from it.

Montagu wasn't particularly concerned about the written history of most of his tannings, only taking issue with one page that recorded him being punished for theft.

He had found his O.T.C. cap badge missing, likely borrowed by another boy and, 'in accordance with custom', he borrowed someone else's to ensure he was not in trouble on Monday morning if found without one. On Saturday, the boy he had borrowed the badge from discovered it missing and Monday brought a demand for answers, which Montagu readily provided. Despite being far from the first instance of a pupil borrowing a badge in this way, it was recorded as theft. Montagu could do little to protest the matter at the time but, with the black book finally in his hands, he tore out the page.

SpitLip's Montagu, who proclaims 'when you write the book, my boy you're off the hook', would probably have approved.

If anything stands as a testament to how personable Ewen Montagu was, it is his family's enduring memory of him and the pride they have for the life he lived. They recall not just the military escapades he wrote about in his books, but the personal stories and tiny details that prove him to still be much talked about and well-remembered, even almost 40 years after his death.

CHAPTER FIVE

HESTER'S FAMILY

OUR research into Hester confirmed the one piece of information that we had known about her before we started: she never married, and she also had no children. When it came to researching her family, we therefore had to turn to her older brothers.

Considering the method of research we had done into Hester had proved successful for us, we started down the same path for her brothers.

The eldest of the three siblings was Donald Hugh Murray Leggatt, sharing a middle name with Hester, and also with William, to honour their mother. Like Hester, he was born in India, specifically in the city of Hyderabad on the 27th May 1899, making him six years older than his sister.

Donald likely didn't see a huge amount of his sister growing up. The 1911 Census reveals him to be at Parkside School in Ewell, Surrey, a preparatory school originally founded in 1879 with only four pupils. At the same time, Hester was still with her parents in India. Same-sex education continued to keep the family separated when Donald began at Charterhouse in 1913, although the friendship between Hester and the daughter of a Charterhouse housemaster, specifically that of Donald's boarding house, does suggest she may have spent some time there.

Charterhouse School, like Wycombe Abbey, Canford and Westminster, keeps excellent archives that record the history of former pupils. We reached out to the Charterhouse archivist and were provided with a wealth of information. Donald's time at Charterhouse was spent living at Gownboys boarding house from Oration Quarter (autumn term) 1913 to Long Quarter (spring term) 1917, and he filled it with plenty to keep himself busy. He was captain of the football First XI, had a place on the cricket First XI, and was involved with the Charterhouse pupil fire brigade.

A couple of years older than Ewen Montagu, Donald did not escape active service in World War One. In 1917 he joined the Royal Navy, serving first as Midshipman on HMS Barham, as well as on the HMS Excellence. Early comments on his Naval Register noted that his knowledge was below the usual standard and that he lacked full understanding of his responsibilities as a commissioned officer. This was put down to his short training – the reality for many recruited in a period of active warfare. It was noted, however, that he was improving quickly and had the potential to develop into a good officer. They also commended his football skills and the strong physique he'd built during his time playing sports at Charterhouse.

His fondness for sports was noted throughout his record, with further comments attesting to his cheerful personality and good leadership qualities. After the war ended, he remained with the Royal Navy, not retiring until 1934, when he'd reached the position of Lieutenant Commander.

In the meantime, Donald had married Valerie Edith Rose De Mattos of Exmouth in a ceremony on the 10th January 1923. Hester was in attendance as a bridesmaid and their brother William served as the best man. Newspapers described the wedding in great detail, with the church decorated in white chrysanthemums, ferns, bamboo foliage and lilies. Valerie wore an ivory charmeuse dress with a train lined with silver gauze and trimmed with orange blossoms.

The bridesmaids' dresses, including the one worn by a then 17-year-old Hester, were meticulously described: Victorian frocks made of silver-shot turquoise taffeta, with frills of silver lace and garlands of pink rosebuds. In addition, each woman wore a matching hat of silver lace, rosebuds, and lengths of narrow silver ribbon falling in curls over the shoulders, with the look completed by silver stockings and shoes, and gold bar brooches, set with aquamarines, as a gift from the groom. If there is one picture we're most sad not to have of Hester, it might be a surviving image from this wedding. This outfit seems like it really needs to be seen to be believed.

Despite a fairy-tale, or at least flower-filled, wedding, and their son born in 1925, Valerie petitioned Donald for divorce after 11 years. The case made the papers owing to the discussions it raised about divorce laws at the time. Donald presented no objection to the petition, and the judge, Sir Boyd Merriman, rejected it, citing collusion between the pair. Merriman emphasised the role of the State in a marriage, and that a union could not be dissolved simply because a couple was 'ill-assorted'.

The records of divorce proceedings between the couple are held in the National Archive, but the documents aren't digitised. Thankfully, a number of our researchers live in London and were able to make the trip to Kew to review the records in person. They concern a second petition for divorce, in 1934. Valerie cited that her request for a divorce was being made on the grounds of 'great neglect and unkindness', and that Donald had committed adultery.

Three instances of adultery were cited, the first with an unknown woman at the Hotel Russell in Russell Square on the 9th and 10th of September 1933, the second with a Norah Reilly at the Grosvenor Hotel on Buckingham

Palace Road on the 23rd and 24th January 1934, and the third was with a woman known to Valerie as Mrs Olive or Mrs Bellaire, lasting from about the 2nd to the 12th of August 1934, after the first divorce petition in 1933.

The documents concerning the divorce revealed an unhappy marriage that had long ended in practice, if not on paper. Valerie requested full custody of their son and, with the pair already living separately, it seems as if Donald was already seeing little if anything of him. In the end, this second divorce petition was granted. Valerie was to receive a lump sum of £358.16.4., a weekly payment of 10 shillings for herself and a further 10 shillings for the maintenance of their son, as well as full custody of him. Given this separation, it seems possible that Hester might not have seen much of her then nine-year-old nephew after this point.

In 1935, Donald remarried Constance Hadfield Olive, presumably the 'Mrs Olive' cited in the divorce petition. She was seven years his senior and, as far as we can tell, this marriage was happier than the first, although it wasn't to last any longer.

In 1939, Donald re-joined the Navy under the shadow of World War Two. Records note him commanding HMS Selkirk, but by July 1942 he was serving at HMS Sphinx, a shore base in Alexandria, Egypt that had been named after a minesweeper lost in an air attack in 1940.

Donald left a particularly strong imprint on the National

Archives, and our visit revealed details of the last few months of his life. On 24th July 1942, a telegram was sent to the Admiralty to report that Commander Donald Hugh Leggatt had been admitted to Addington Hospital, Durban and placed on the seriously ill list, suffering from ascites, or the build-up of fluid in the abdomen.

Further telegrams were sent on 31st July, 7th August, 14th August, 21st August, 29th August, 5th September, and 18th September, all reporting his condition to be unchanged. On 22nd September, the message finally changed, and not for the better.

Donald died of natural causes that were determined to be unattributable to and not aggravated by his naval service. A telegram to Constance Leggatt, Donald's second wife, specifies the cause as 'carcinoma of caecum, liver and pancreas.' He was buried at Stellawood Military Cemetery, Durban, South Africa, with an inscription reading 'In Proud and Loving Memory', leaving behind a widow and one son. This was seven months before Hester worked on Operation Mincemeat.

Whether it was connected to his service or not, he died during wartime active service and was buried far from home, never returning to his family. Hester had first-hand experience of the loss of a serving family member. Diana, the fictitious little sister from the *Operation Mincemeat* musical's *Dear Bill* who eagerly awaits her brother's return, might have been young and naïve, but no doubt the real

Hester would have been able to relate to her hope and how it would be crushed. No one wants to believe their loved ones will never come home.

If there was one thing the story of Operation Mincemeat was not lacking, it was more Williams, but unfortunately the Leggatt family were rather enamoured with the name. The closest William to Hester was her second brother, born September 2nd 1900 in Fife, Scotland. Like his older brother, he was attending Parkside School in Surrey by 1911, but, unlike Donald and for reasons that continue to elude us, William did not attend Charterhouse and instead found himself at Winchester. Fortunately, they also have excellent archives.

Like his brother, William was a sportsman at school. He attended from September 1914 to December 1918, boarding in Du Boulay's House and playing on the cricket First XI and the football First XI. Considering the frequency with which public school sports teams play against each other, it is possible he faced off against Donald if their tenures on their respective teams overlapped. Not content with eleven-a-side football games, he also played on his house six-a-side football team, of which he was captain in 1918. The writer of his Winchester School obituary recorded that he would 'never forget an exhibition of kicking' given by William.

William kept up both cricket and football even after he left school. He went on to Royal Military Academy

Woolwich, where he was captain of both their cricket and football teams. He won two cricket matches played against Royal Military College, Sandhurst. In 1920, he played a game of football against Westminster School, winning 5-1. While it would be fair to say these victories were not his alone and that the success ought to be shared by the 10 other members of each team, William had an indisputable talent. He played cricket for Kent in 1926, as well as for the Army in 1926 and every year from 1930 to 1934. Of the 11 first-class matches we know him to have played in, five were for Kent and six were for the British Army.

In July 1929, William married Connel Auld Mathieson of Glasgow, Scotland. The wedding was held at St Columba's Church in London and, while we haven't found a detailed description of the dress she would have been wearing, it seems likely that Hester would have been in attendance, if not a bridesmaid, just as she was for Donald's wedding. William's marriage certainly lasted longer than either of his brother's. He and Connel had four children: Michael William Leggatt (born 1931), Jocelyn Mary Connel Leggatt (born 1933), and twins Anthea Jane Leggatt and Susan A Leggatt (both born 1936).

An obituary found for Michael, the oldest child, revealed him to be 'an avid and prolific writer of letters'. Considering Hester's role writing 'Pam's' love letters in Operation Mincemeat, this piece of information seemed particularly sentimental.

Regardless of how coincidental, the increasing number of links we found to both Hester herself and the *Operation Mincemeat* musical were warmly received in the Minceflu-encer Discord server, where all new discoveries were still being reported.

William stayed with the army between the wars, promoted to Captain in 1933. He served as an instructor at Sandhurst from 1931 to 1935. After his stint teaching, he served as a Brigade Major in Egypt, not far from where his brother would die a few years later.

In 1942, William was commanding the 11th Regiment Royal Horse Artillery in North Africa. He fought at the Battle of El Alamein, for which he was awarded a Distinguished Service Order. The recommendation cited that 'Lt. Col. Leggatt spent the day… with the leading tanks, under heavy shell fire, advising and encouraging the young officers around him…', and '…after constant heavy fighting and casualties to personnel, the regiment was still fighting 24 guns. This was due entirely to Lt. Col. Leggatt's… personal example he set to the ranks.'

Hester knew the work she was doing in the War Office would have serious ramifications for military personnel, but she might not have known just how personal her efforts had become. She didn't tell her brothers about the details of her work, something that frustrated them, so perhaps William equally didn't share the details of his, but his regiment would be the first guns ashore in the invasion of Sicily. This was the very invasion Operation Mincemeat was designed to support, drawing Nazi forces away from the island with the fictitious plans to invade Sardinia instead.

Thanks in part to the work of the Operation Mincemeat team, the invasion of Sicily was a success and casualty numbers were far lower than they might otherwise have been. William made it out alive. Whether Hester ever told him that she had helped in the mission to safeguard his life and the lives of his fellow soldiers, we may never know, but she didn't have many years in which to do it.

In August 1943, William took up command of the 83rd Anti-Tank Regiment, but by May 1944 he returned to England due to ill health. He was placed on a year's sick leave in April 1945, but never recovered. On 13th August 1946, he suffered a heart attack in the smoking room of the Cavalry Club, 127 Piccadilly, a gentleman's club that still exists, now under the name The Cavalry and Guards Club. The heart attack was deemed to be an extended result of his military service. He was buried on 17th August in the churchyard at Hinton St. George Church-yard, Somerset.

By the time William passed away, Hester had already lost Donald and her father, who had died in 1935. Just one year later, on 26th June 1947, Hester's mother would also pass away. The two were living together at the time so we can assume they were close. One year later, the electoral

registers show that Hester had moved from the accommodation they'd shared at 102 Queens Gate, South Kensington, to 2 Gledhow Gardens, Chelsea.

This final death would leave Hester with no immediate
family whatsoever, for the rest of her life.

CHAPTER SIX

FINDING LIVING LEGGATTS

JACK LAWRENCE

THE Montagu family had been fans of the musical from the very beginning and Colonel Bevan's descendants had also given their approval, but no one had ever heard from the Leggatts. If there were any out there, they hadn't made themselves known to the team at *Operation Mincemeat* and there was a good chance they didn't know about the show at all.

The families of Montagu and Bevan still felt connected to the men's stories; close relatives remembered family tales and had clothing and documents belonging to them. One of Bevan's descendants wore his trousers to the show's Gala Night, and Montagu's family gifted Natasha one of his hats.

If there were any related Leggatts out there, they weren't direct descendants of Hester, as she never had any children of her own, but both of her brothers had married and started families. She had nieces and nephews, who went on to have children of their own. These family lines would be her closest relations. If anyone remembered her at all, it would be them. We just needed to find them.

One member of the Discord had been following the #FindingHester project from the beginning during its early stages, but didn't have much experience with historical research or genealogy. He wanted to get involved but knew he'd be far better at finding living people rather than the dead. When Hester's family tree started to come together, he began to wonder about living family members, and whether they would be happy to talk to the bunch of weirdos who had dedicatedly been researching their relative, someone not related to any of us and who had been dead nearly 30 years. The gap on the team had presented itself and he filled it perfectly.

All but the most careful of us leave traces of information about ourselves on the internet, often without realising it. Collecting and piecing together these digital breadcrumbs requires practice, effort, and a bit of luck. This process, known as open source intelligence (OSINT) gathering, is practiced by private investigators, war crimes experts, journalists, intelligence agencies... and the newest member of team #FindingHester.

He had once tracked down the contact details for a man his friend met at a bar one night based on nothing beyond his extremely common first name, a physical description, and the city he lived in. His friend and the man had hit it off over drinks but forgot to exchange numbers. Both were delighted, if mildly terrified, when he was able to put them back in touch. That delight was what we were hoping to inspire in any living Leggatts we could find, but hopefully with minimal terror.

Setting out to find out everything he could about Hester's brothers, the researcher started with William. The name the Operation Mincemeat team gave to their corpse and the name of the American pilot who landed in the same spot just before the corpse was deployed, William was already a common name in this tale even before adding Hester's brother to the mix. An initial Google search revealed a haunting new development: not only is William a common name on its own, there are a huge number of William Leggatts out there.

Going through every result would be impossible and reducing the search to 'William M. Leggatt' wasn't much help either, not bringing up anything new. Most people aren't out there using their middle name with much frequency, but without it, it just wasn't possible to know which William Leggatt was the right one. Once page 10 of the Google search results was reached, it was time to change tack.

We had already established from William Leggatt's obituary that he had four children, the oldest of which was Michael William. We were relieved to see William relegated to middle name status and our luck only continued, finally unearthing something useful.

On a website that still carries a warning in our research notes for being dodgy, a pdf of the May 2014 edition of the Winchester College Alumni magazine, *The Trusty Servant*, contained Michael's obituary. He had, as many public school pupils do, followed in his father's footsteps and attended the same school. Michael had passed away in 2013, survived by a son and a daughter. While lacking details about his daughter, his son was identified with the initials WKCL and included the years he'd attended Winchester himself, narrowing down a rough age.

It didn't seem sensible to waste much time on considering all the possible options for what the 'W' in WKCL might stand for. Because it was this story and this family, William seemed like a safe bet.

So we were back to another William Leggatt, but now we had a much narrower age bracket. Surely this would be easier. He was the right age to likely have a social media platform of some kind, or at least some substantial internet presence. He had no reason to hide away, not knowing a researcher would one day be tracking him down owing to an investigation into the war work of his great aunt.

Not one of us had ever heard the name William Leggatt

in our lives, but when our researcher trawled across half a dozen social media sites, he still ended up with a list of over 100 possible matches. That was before nicknames had even been considered, with plenty more Wills, Bills and Billys out there. There really are far more William Leggatts than you'd think possible.

Not one to be deterred from tracking down women in history because they weren't talked about as much as men, the team used birth records to track down Michael William Leggatt's daughter, who had gone unnamed in his obituary. She turned out to be Anthea, who shares a name with one of her father's sisters, causing a little bit more confusion to add to the William debacle. If you ever want to stop a strange theatre fandom from tracking down your entire family history, giving everyone the same name is an excellent way of putting most people off. Team #FindingHester was not most people.

A potential address had been found for Anthea, Hester's niece, but there was no way of knowing if she still lived there. Perhaps it would be possible to do one better for William Leggatt and track down a contact number.

After excluding any William Leggatts with completely blank profiles or no links to the United Kingdom, about 50 candidates still remained. Narrowing this list down further took our researcher the best part of a day, but he eventually identified a likely candidate. This William ran an IT and communications company and, while a little younger than estimated, still seemed plausible. So, an email was drafted.

'Hi William,' it started. 'Sorry to email you out of the blue. I hope this email finds you well. Was your late father the nephew of Hester Leggatt? She was a secretary in MI5 during World War Two and played an important role in the Operation Mincemeat military deception scheme, saving thousands of soldiers' lives in the process and helping win the war.' This was followed with a quick summary of who we were and what on earth we were doing, and off it was sent.

This first William Leggatt responded just three hours later, enthusiastic but tentative. He was 'not sure' if he was the right person, and his father had only died the previous year, not adding up with the Winchester magazine obituary. After a brief back and forth it became clear that this was, indeed, an incorrect William. The research-er thanked him for his time and sent him a link to the *Operation Mincemeat* ticket booking page, just in case he was ever in London and in want of a good night out at the theatre.

An hour later, another email went out; this William Leggatt lived in Brighton, was a 3D artist, and went by Will. 'Hello Will,' the email began and continued identi-cally to the previous one. Two hours later, the next reply came: this was another case of mistaken identity, 'I believe they must be from an entirely different family of Leggatts,' as he put it. Moreover, this William Leggatt's father was still alive. This second William Leggatt was wished a good weekend and also sent a link to the *Operation Mincemeat* show ticket page. 'Tickets are cheapest on Monday', was helpfully added.

It was 5pm on a Friday afternoon by this point and the researcher had already cold-emailed two William Leggatts who weren't the William Leggatt he was after. Rather than emailing every single William Leggatt on the list of possibilities, he refocused and spent the next 24 hours refining the list down as far as possible. By the next day, the name William Leggatt no longer seemed real, but one candidate had risen to the top. This William Leggatt worked for a chemical conglomerate and his picture on LinkedIn bore a striking resemblance to the other Leggatts we had historical images of. Unfortunately, this third William Leggatt had no publicly available email address.

Not one to be deterred by something as simple as that, the researcher emailed the press contact for his company with a request that the same email previously sent to two other contenders please be forwarded to this new Mr William Leggatt. This was 6.22 on a Saturday evening after a day of intense research, so he went to bed expecting to hear nothing further that weekend.

After a busy few hours at work on Sunday morning and while running errands on his lunch break, his phone rang. The number was unknown and so the answer was fairly resigned, in expectation of a cold caller. 'It's William Leggatt here. I believe you're looking for me,' a male voice said. The phone was dropped to the floor in shock.

Our researcher scrambled to retrieve his phone and paced his way through a conversation where Will, as he preferred to be known, confirmed he'd received the email and wasn't entirely sure whether he was the correct William Leggatt, but thought he might be. After some genealogical questions to confirm things, it became apparent that a hectic week of searching had paid off. This was finally the correct man, and the rest of the William Leggatts out there were finally safe from confusing emails about a funny little World War Two musical.

Will was pleased to hear about our research and had been unaware of Hester's full involvement in Operation Mincemeat. He recalled hearing vague details about her but could not definitively confirm anything beyond his relation to Hester. He mentioned he could put us in touch with Anthea, the niece we'd found record of only recently before, via her son Bill. Because if there was one thing this story was lacking, it was some extra Williams.

This was exciting, tangible, *real* progress. We had found Hester's living relatives and were a step closer to finding Hester herself. Messages to other #FindingHester team members were a jumbled mess of 'ITS RHE RIGHT ONE' (typo and all), followed up with 'HE HQS

ABRHEATHW FEYQIKE.' The researcher maintains this was an attempt at 'he has Anthea's details,' before his brain had kicked back into normal working function.

Will made good on his promise to loop Bill into matters, who confirmed in his first email that:

'Historians have spelt Leggatt incorrectly. As Will said, you've got the right woman.'

The email continued: 'My Mum, Anthea (née Leggatt), and I watched the Colin Firth film not too long ago – and halfway through, Mum chips in with "she was my Aunt, you know," which blew my mind. I'd forgotten Mum telling me decades ago about her Aunt who wrote the fake-girlfriend letters in some WW2 book.'

Bill also revealed that his wife Linda had met Hester shortly before she died in 1995, 'but there were no war stories or memorable conversations.'

Bill recalls being amazed, excited and strangely proud to know that there was a group of strangers so interested in a fairly distant family member. He was excited to find out how much research we had managed to do, and was proud to share DNA with Hester. Some of his amazement was regarding the musical itself, intrigued that someone had made a hit musical from the plot of Operation Mincemeat. We were all incredibly keen for the Leggatt family to see the show for themselves, to see Hester portrayed so excellently and so carefully by Jak.

Bill and Will were put in touch with the producers of

Operation Mincemeat, in the hopes that they could go and see it the way some of the other families had. To our delight, they were offered the opportunity and began discussing mutually agreeable dates. Will was eager for his children to join, and Bill asked if his wife could come too, saying, 'She will divorce me if I go without her.' Thankfully no divorces were risked for the sake of the show and tickets were issued for a whole host of Leggatts to come and see a performance.

One night in August, just over 28 years after Hester died, her family and a small group of #FindingHester researchers met at Nell of Old Drury in Covent Garden, a pub named after Nell Gwyn, mistress of King Charles II. The pub reportedly had a tunnel that links it to the Theatre Royal Drury Lane across the road, but no one actually knows where it is anymore. Still, the connection to the world of theatre felt apt.

We gathered upstairs, nervously awaiting the arrival of the Leggatts. It had not escaped any of us that our research project could be considered to some as entirely mad, and that the Leggatts might be somewhat wary of meeting with a group of people who had been rather obsessively researching one of their deceased relatives.

Thankfully, they were forgiving of the latent madness of it all and instead chatted with us about our research. The room above the pub quickly became lively, the nerves melting away, as we broke into small groups with members of the family to discuss what we'd discovered. We showed them photographs and explained the avenues of research we still wanted to explore. In return, they shared what they knew of Hester, admitting it was very little.

We surprised the family with our numbers, and with the variance of ages between us. For many, the kind of genealogical research we had been doing is a pastime picked up later in life, when people find themselves with extra free time, but we were a motley crew from all walks of life and generations.

The meet-up concluded with a group photograph of the assembled researchers and family members. One of the daughters of Hester's great nephew had to be summoned across the room by her full name to join in. Hearing the name Leggatt aloud, used to refer to an actual person who was actually related to Hester was one of the moments when it all felt the most real. These were Leggatts and, thanks to the hard work of an incredibly skilled researcher, we had found them and brought them together, with the children of the two sides of the family never having met before. They exchanged social media accounts while we were all there, so they could stay in touch. If nothing else, we had achieved this.

We all watched the show that night with a desperate hope that the Leggatts would like it. Their female relative was being played by a man in a comedy musical about one of the weirdest stories to come out of World War Two, so there were no guarantees.

When the show ended, we reconvened in a rainy alleyway next to the theatre, a sea of umbrellas. While we waited for the cast to recover from the show, Montagu's great-grandson, who had also been there to see the show, met some of the Leggatts. It was another one of those mundane but incomprehensible moments, the meeting of the descendants of two people who had known each other generations ago. Something Montagu and Hester would have found baffling, no doubt, especially considering the story that had gotten us to that point.

Thankfully, Hester's family had enjoyed the show. In some ways they'd known what they were letting themselves in for from the beginning, aware of the gender-blind casting and the multi-roling done by a small cast. In many other ways, they had no idea what to expect at all. Before seeing the show for themselves, they couldn't quite understand how we could be so invested in it as to have spent so much time researching one of its characters.

Even those amongst their numbers who were not the biggest fans of musicals were won over from the start of the first song. There is something special at the heart of this show, whether you're related to one of the characters or not, and, as one of Hester's family members can attest, it can change your opinion about musicals forever.

Meeting the Leggatt family after the show that night

was a significant moment for Jak Malone. He had always assumed there were probably Leggatts out there somewhere, but had never dreamed that we would be able to locate them, even as we started our research. He had felt like he was carrying her memory alone, until he got to discuss her with them on that rainy evening in the alleyway, next to where he brought her to life every night for 432 people.

The next day, both sides of the family reached out with their feedback of the night. Will's email read:

It was great to meet the team that has done all the research and the actors themselves, and even better to see the musical. They have certainly found something totally different with their (pretty bonkers and very funny) interpretation, giving different points of view from just the standard establishment perspective.

Bill agreed adding:

We LOVED the show and it was so nice to meet everyone involved. I can't wait to show Mum the photos of Hester and Donald, and all the photos from last night.

After meeting the cast at the stage door, Hester's family and a small group of the Finding Hester researchers went out for one last pint at another nearby pub. As the discussion turned towards Hester, Bill's wife, Linda, told us about her memories of meeting Hester in the nursing home she lived in towards the end of her life. She described Hester as a sweet old lady who asked far more questions than she answered and never brought up her work on Operation Mincemeat.

In a funny coincidence, cast member Seán Carey, who was the first cover Cholmondeley and second cover Hester at the time, was passing through the pub and also got to meet the Leggatts and discussed Hester and her importance to history and the show. He would go on to tell her story several times before the end of the first year's contract, after which he became principal Cholmondeley. He no longer gets to cover Hester, but he's still a piece of her enduring story.

The night ended with goodbyes and promises to stay in touch from both sides: we weren't done with our research, and we hoped we'd have more to share with them in due course. The connections made and strengthened between Hester's family and the #FindingHester team would prove to be invaluable in the coming months. It was with a renewed vigour that we dived back into our research attempts.

ADDITIONAL RESEARCH: FINDING HASELDEN

ROSE CROSSGROVE

HASELDEN appears unceremoniously early in Act Two of *Operation Mincemeat*, pushing a desk on stage and settling under a slowly rotating fan, glowing vigorously from the Spanish sun and his efforts. He breaks the news of the Allied pilot Willie Watkins' crash and the arrival of Montagu and Cholmondeley's stolen corpse. Throughout his time on stage, he appears as well-meaning, if somewhat out of his depth, as the threads begin to unravel and parts of the deception are put at risk. All of the characters in the show are to some degree used for comic effect, considering it is, of course, a comedy, but the ineptness of SpitLip's Haselden is an emphasised source of humour.

Tasked with overseeing the autopsy of the corpse, Haselden introduces himself as being from the consulate, and makes some vague references to previous missions elsewhere in Europe with limited success. In a pep talk he gives to himself he insists that 'you cannot let His Majesty down. Not again. Not after... Helsinki.' The audience is left to wonder what exactly did happen in Finland. The answer is nothing, as it turns out. SpitLip just thought it was an appropriately amusing place name for the line.

Haselden continues his role of comic relief as the stakes rise in the Second Act, but he is also central to the success of the plan. Without Haselden, there is no way to get the documents into the right hands. Montagu, in particular, is unconvinced by his skills. In the end, he succeeds, despite some confusion, in getting the documents into the hands of the German agents.

Francis Kinnaird Haselden, the real man behind the character, shared a much deeper connection with the town of Huelva. His long-standing relationship with the region changed with life under both Franco's rule and the ever-growing Nazi presence from the end of the 1930s. The information here about Haselden's life comes from a mix of documents obtained through sources such as electoral records, departure lists and parish records, references in the Mincemeat archives at the Imperial War Museum and National Archives. It also draws from historical works on the presence and work of British Counterintelligence in Huelva throughout World War Two. Bringing them together here provides depth to a man whose life changed dramatically under Franco's regime and who chose to risk his own life and position to support different Allied efforts during the war.

The British presence in Huelva has a commercial history and a community of British mining engineers and their families grew in the region linked to their interest in the local resources. A large number of British companies, including Rio Tinto and Tharsis were heavily involved in pyrite mining around the Andalucian province of Huelva from the 19th century onwards. In the La Caroline area, the (New) Centenillo Silver Lead Mines were under the purview of Henry Haselden from 1886 onwards. Francis was the son of Henry Adolphus and Kate Haselden (nee Rippin). He was born around July of 1882 in Linares, Spain. It's likely this was due to the mines operated by his father in and around this region. He was baptised on 30th September 1882 in New Brentford, along with his twin sister Elsie. His father's profession is given as engineer; thus the family's life in Spain was linked to the mine operated by the family.

Due to the family's presence in Spain, it is difficult to access much information about Francis Haselden's early life. It's likely he spent a lot of time outside of England even as a young man, as he and the rest of the family do not seem to appear in the 1891, 1901 or 1911 census. The children of these sorts of families would likely have been educated in England at this time, but without a location from the census it's difficult to say whether this was the case for Francis. However, during this time he followed in his father's footsteps and became an engineer in his own right.

Records do show the Haselden family (without Francis) travelling to London from Gibraltar in July 1909 and this reflects evidence from passenger manifests through-out the early 20th century of movement between, for the most part, England and Spain for Francis Haselden and his family. Haselden himself travelled from Malta to Plymouth, landing on the 21st June 1913. This trip was a special one; heading back to England for his wedding. He married Mary Jean Henderson (b.1894) in the Parish of Finchley on 6th July 1913. There are records of seven children born to the couple between 1914 and 1930, the majority of whom were born in Huelva, Spain. Five of their seven children survived to adulthood.

Numerous passenger records indicate Haselden continued to move back and forth between Spain and England through the 1910s and 1920s, with records showing a trip to Lisbon in December of 1918 and a return to England on 1st August 1935. There are medal records for a Francis Haselden serving in the French theatre during World War One, but it seems likely that this is Francis Edward Haselden, who though coincidentally also born in 1882, seems to have been no relation.

Several of his children also made frequent similar journeys during this time to attend boarding schools in England, including his sons David and Ian at Weymouth College and daughter Helen at Uplands School. According to the records of the Foreign Office List and Diplomatic and Consular Year Book 1953, Francis Haselden served as pro-consul at Huelva from 26th August 1919, in addition to his work in the mines.

It is easy to forget when focussing on the events of World War Two and the ways in which the lives of so many were irrevocably changed by the period of the late 1930s through the 1940s, that Spain had already undergone a devastating civil war. This conflict started with an attempted military coup in July 1936. Following a narrow victory by Republican left-wing parties in the elections, the Nationalists chose to attempt to overthrow the Spanish Republic, rather than take control in government. With the backing of Mussolini in Italy, Nationalist military leaders attempted to take control of military districts within Spain, but failed to take any major cities except Seville.

The conflict continued to April of 1939 with eventual victory for the Nationalist forces and bloody reprisals for the Republicans. In the end Francisco Franco Bahamonde was declared 'Caudillo de España' from 1938 and remained in that position until 1973, operating as dictator of Spain. Resistance from the Maquis groups continued until the 1960s, and operated in support of Allied forces up to 1945. Despite the support from Italy and Germany for the Nationalist forces during the civil war, Spain declared official neutrality in World War Two.

Haselden and family remained in Spain under the Franco regime and stayed in Huelva throughout the 1930s and 1940s. According to Foreign Office records, Haselden served as Acting Consul in Huelva in 1934, 1936 and 1938. On 18th November, 1939, Francis Haselden was appointed as the British Vice Consul in Huelva following the death of his predecessor, cementing a formal relationship with the British Government during the war.

From the late 1930s onwards, Haselden ran an underground network in contact with Seville, Gibraltar and London. During World War Two, Haselden and his network were involved in counterespionage around enemy activities in the region. They provided information about enemy action, helping escaped Allied pilots, soldiers and prisoners of war to safety. Haselden transmitted encrypted messages using the telegraphic addresses *Shipminder* in London and *Drawbridge* in Gibraltar, code names for English Intelligence offices. The network also fulfilled an important anti-sabotage role and monitored the activities of the Italian ship *Gaeta* and its proposed intelligence activities during 1943. These activities ran primarily out of Haselden's own house at 36 Generalísimo Franco Street (now Marina Street), in which the lower floor was used as the offices of the vice-consulate and his own business.

Among his collaborators were Robert Sinclair and Albert Shutte. These men were both also part of the local British mining community, working for the Tharsis and Rio Tinto Company respectively. Sinclair also took over as British pro-consul in the city. The presence of the long-standing existing communities of resident foreigners in Huelva allowed intelligence networks to form quickly. Adolf Clauss, a notable local Abwehr (German military intelligence) agent, came too from the immigrant mining community in Huelva, on the German side, which had existed alongside and with frequent collaboration with the British companies since the 19th century.

Haselden's role in Operation Mincemeat was significant in verifying the false identity of Major Martin and he was one of the only people on the ground in Huelva to be aware that an operation was taking place. Due to his long-standing relationship to the town, it would have been extremely difficult to undertake the mission without Haselden's knowledge, though exactly how much information he was given is difficult to ascertain.

According to Haselden's daughter Elizabeth, prior to the commencement of Mincemeat in Spain, her father was concerned with the weather conditions; the body arrived a day later than expected and was delayed by the local fishing crews. Even Haselden's close accomplices in counterespionage were not informed of the plot, to reduce any risk of leaks to the Spanish or German agents.

Haselden was instructed to notify Anglo-Spanish naval attaché Salvador 'Don' Gómez-Beare at the Madrid embassy and then arrange for the burial of the body. Gómez-Beare would continue the communications about any lost bag or papers via both the telephone and cable to seed the idea of British concern via the known German intercepts on these communication lines. Haselden was instructed to make enquiries for the missing documents, but to make sure not to retrieve them before the Germans had a chance to get a look.

Haselden was present at the docks to accompany the body to the cemetery. Also present were Lt. Pascual del Pobil, the naval judge, Dr Eduardo Fernández del Torno and his son Dr. Eduardo Fernández Contioso and recently crashed U.S. pilot Willie Watkins. The effects were removed from Glyndwr Michael's body and the briefcase opened. Lt Pascual del Pobil then offered the documents to Haselden immediately, which Haselden then had to fall back on procedure and official channels to refuse. Haselden went so far as to make himself absent for a time, so he could not be offered the documents for a second time, taking an hours long bus journey from Damas to Seville and earning the ire of the local British community for not dealing with the body immediately.

Haselden was also present at the autopsy of the body,

and aimed to motivate the least detailed report possible. The internal state of the body encouraged the doctors present to agree and certify a drowning following a crash. Haselden then cabled Gómez-Beare to confirm the identity of the body and the funeral to follow that Sunday, 2nd May 1943. This was to encourage the interception of the documents by Adolf Clauss and his network by alerting them further to specific British interest in this particular marine.

Haselden was in attendance at the funeral, along with local British and Free French representatives and Lt. Pascual del Pobil. Haselden arranged for the burial costs to be covered and moved quickly to avoid any further questions or the possibility of a second autopsy. The British consulate then contracted to pay the rental and maintenance costs of the grave in perpetuity.

The Spanish navy initially followed proper channels and refused to give the German agents access to the documents. Haselden was instructed to make further investigations into where the papers had ended up. On 5th May 1943, he was informed that the documents were being handed over to Cádiz; Clauss was informed of the same. Haselden then passed on this information, which was sent on to London with notes of great concern over the lost documents and their whereabouts.

In worlds of espionage and counterespionage, even those in charge of operations would not necessarily be aware of the positions of those involved in aspects of their operation. The letters of Ewen Montagu reveal a scepticism towards Haselden and his involvement. In a 1969 letter from the collection held by the Imperial War Museum, Montagu claimed Haselden was entirely unaware of Mincemeat and that the ambassador, Samuel Hoare, had forbidden the use of regional diplomats in espionage in Spain. Montagu also refers to a quote Haselden gave to a previous book on the Mincemeat operation that nothing would have gone on without him 'being in it' with no minor level of doubt.

Mincemeat had to operate alongside and without knowledge of any other intelligence activities in Huelva and more widely across Spain. Given the position Haselden actually occupied within the local counterintelligence networks, it seems more likely that Haselden was, as he later stated, aware of Mincemeat and his role within it. Given the need to draw the attention of the local Abwehr agents and his knowledge of their networks it would make sense for Haselden to be briefed, and for Montagu to be unaware, to protect other British intelligence interests in Huelva.

A capacity for intelligence work seems to have been a hallmark of the Haselden family during the war. Haselden's eldest surviving daughter Helen appears in Government Code and Cypher School (GC&CS) records compiled by a GCHQ historian as a temporary typist during the Abyssinia (Ethiopia) crisis in 1935. What was a temporary post as a 19-year-old seems to have turned into a career. Helen can later be found on the 1939 Register at 97 Victoria Road in Bletchley, where she lists her occupation as Civil Servant.

According to the Bletchley Park roll of honour, Helen (or Margaret as she seems to have been known to the family) served throughout the war, first at Broadway and then at Bletchley Park. Helen having any involvement in passing on information around the troop movements in Sicily seems unlikely, but the very faint possibility remains that at some point she may have been working with her own father's information.

The final piece comes through a lacuna in the documentation – a list of wartime civilian staff from GC&CS in which her name is conspicuously absent. Several others who were known to have remained with GCHQ following the war also do not appear on the wartime service lists. The newly renamed GCHQ returned to London in 1946 and moved to Cheltenham in 1951. Helen returned to London in 1946 and remained there until at least 1953, living in Fulham. She then found herself in Cheltenham, with the rest of the family, in the late 1950s.

Francis Haselden was awarded an OBE in the New Year's Honours 1953, likely as a result of his work in Spain. He seems to have retired at this point from his work and moved back to England settling first in Coulsden,

Surrey and then more permanently in Cheltenham, Gloucestershire. Francis Kinnaird Haselden died on the 11th December 1964 leaving a bequest and the house he had settled in to his children.

CHAPTER SEVEN

PICTURE THE SCENE

ONE of the things we most wanted to uncover in our search for Hester, especially as we got to learn more about her, was a photograph.

We knew what Ewen Montagu and Charles Cholmondeley looked like, with both of their images readily available in media that discusses Operation Mincemeat. Jean Leslie's image is almost synonymous with the name of the operation, with a photograph of her holding a towel at the beach being included in the briefcase as evidence of the existence of 'Pam', the fiancée. But Hester wrote the letters, leaving us with an image of her handwriting, but not her face.

Her appearance certainly matters less than what she did, but we were still keen to see what this woman we had spent so long researching actually looked like.

Especially if it put the final nail in the coffin of the elderly Hester myth.

We started with the only image we had available to us that might conceivably contain Hester: a group photograph of the staff of Section 17M, Montagu's division of Naval Intelligence. Taken in Room 13 in the Admiralty basement, in front of walls papered with maps, seven women stand behind five seated men, with Montagu himself clearly identifiable towards the centre.

It would have been so wonderfully simple to be able to point to one of those women and know she was Hester, but unfortunately this was to be the part of our research that caused us the most trouble. None of these women were Hester. Two could be confirmed as Juliette Ponsonby and Patricia Trehearne, but the five remaining candidates couldn't be ruled out until we found a copy of the photograph in Ewen Montagu's papers at the Imperial War Museum. Underneath the image are all the signatures of the individuals pictured. It isn't clear which name applies to which person, but none of them read 'Hester Leggatt'.

Hester was not a part of 17M. Unlike the recent film suggests, she did not work directly for Montagu and was actually employed as a Grade 2 administrative assistant in section B1A. This role had her working alongside those in charge of the Double Cross operations, which likely did see her interacting with Montagu, who served as the

Naval Representative on the XX Committee. This is how she became involved in Operation Mincemeat.

With the one potential Operation Mincemeat-linked image ruled out as a source for a photograph of Hester, we made sure to follow any potential avenue to find one during our research. Our biggest hope had been that her family might have held on to pictures, but those we got in touch with had only met her at the very end of her life, if at all. They had taken no photographs themselves and any that Hester might have owned don't seem to have survived.

When we uncovered the newspaper articles of Esme Langton and Geoffrey Greig's wedding, they were accompanied by images. These photographs are scans from already grainy newspaper print and the quality is not high, but one did contain the entire wedding party, and we knew from the text of the article that Hester had been a bridesmaid. The only question was, which one was she?

The bride is clearly identifiable at the centre of the image, but that left seven other women and girls in the picture to rule out. Hester was 22 at the time of the wedding, so it was easy to rule out the four youngest on the right-hand side. The two smallest were Patricia Hollowell and Audrey Fletcher, both four years old and daughters of Charterhouse masters, dressed in little replicas of Esme's wedding dress to serve as her train bearers, as described in the newspaper article. Diana Thatcher, aged seven, was the daughter of the organist at the wedding, who was once employed by Charterhouse before defecting to Harrow. Jane Smart, aged 11 and yet another daughter of a Charterhouse master, is the only age-appropriate identification for the final young attendant. She also grew up to serve as a secretary at the War Office in World War Two.

The article provided only the names of each of the bridesmaids and train bearers, sending us on mini research trips to identify each girl and match her name to her, ruling individuals out one after the other. With the four youngest members of the wedding party clearly not Hester, we were left with three names: Helen Raxworthy, Patricia Evans, and Hester herself.

Researching Patricia revealed her to be Esme's cousin, born in 1911. With nothing else to go on, we compared the three women that remained and came to an agreement that one of them was clearly younger, making her likely to be 17-year-old Patricia.

And then there were two.

Hester was 22 in the photograph and her fellow remaining bridesmaid, Helen, was 27. The five-year gap, combined with the poor quality of the image, did not provide us with a huge amount to go on when trying to discern a match for Hester. Ultimately, all we could do was make a well-informed guess.

In news articles about the wedding, Hester is consistently named first in the list of bridesmaids. This suggests that she was serving as the maid-of-honour, as she would not have been first alphabetically, by either first name or last, or by age. One of the two remaining candidates in the image is standing next to the bride, turned towards her, just as the best man, Brian Hewitt, flanks the groom on the opposite side. With this as our working theory, we showed the image to a member of the Leggatt family, who identified a resemblance between this woman and Hester's niece in her youth.

This left us with an image that was *probably* Hester, although we could hardly make any guarantees. Even if this was her, the image was grainy and poor quality. The other image from the wedding that included members of the wedding party was even worse, although it seems the woman walking beside the best man is likely Hester. If she was, as we believed, functioning as a maid of honour, it made sense that she would be accompanied by Brian Hewitt, as the first couple in the wedding procession.

The photographs had gone through the process of being printed on cheap newspaper and then digitised in enough quality to be functionally legible, but were by no means high definition. So we made efforts to track down higher quality versions. However, attempts to contact the newspaper archives and organisations that may have held collections of the photographer's work were unsuccessful. We hope there are photographs of the wedding out there somewhere, held by family members of Esme and

Geoffrey, that might one day be uncovered. If nothing else, the details of the bridesmaids' dresses deserve to be seen in all their questionable glory.

It probably comes as no surprise that we were not entirely content with two grainy images of someone that was just more likely Hester than not. Considering their generosity in helping with our research, we turned back to Wycombe Abbey in search of an earlier photograph from her time at the school.

The institution of the yearly school photograph is not a new one. Everyone is familiar with the process of getting organised into height order and filing into neat lines, with some people standing, some kneeling, and some unlucky enough to be sitting on the floor. This is a time-honoured experience, with a history almost as old as the advent of photography itself. School archives often contain group photographs of school houses, sports teams, year groups and individual classes, as well as the occasional whole school photograph. We were optimistic when we reached out to Wycombe Abbey. If Hester had been at the school for more than four years, it seemed impossible for her to have avoided every potential group photograph. We just had to hope that at least one she was in had survived in the archive.

It was the Barry House photographs that were most likely to have caught Hester. Two existed from her time at the school: one from 1920, depicting the entirety of the

House; and one from 1922, likely depicting Barry House officers and monitors. We knew from Hester's own record of her time at the school that she had been both a House Monitor and House Editor, so she could have earned her place in this second image.

Neither photograph comes with a helpful caption of names. We have no concrete guarantee that Hester is in either. While she certainly should be in at least the whole House photograph and she was House Editor by 1922, a still slightly amorphous role that we assumed qualified her for inclusion in the photograph of House officers, there was no list of people in the photographs. Hester could have been unwell, purposefully avoiding picture day, or otherwise engaged. Hoping that wasn't the case, we set to work with the tools we did have at our disposal: images of her brothers.

Thankfully, William Leggatt's Winchester College photographs came with captions. We had an uninterrupted series of each year from 1915 to 1918, with him identified in each one. Ironically, the 1915 caption had his name spelt 'Leggett', suggesting the misspelling was something that plagued more than one of the Leggatt siblings. The series of four photographs of William show a young boy growing up, but he is recognisable throughout.

Donald Leggatt's school photographs from Charterhouse suffer the same fate as Hester's, in that they are without names. The Charterhouse archivist provided three images that should have included Donald, based on the activities he was known to have taken part in: a 1915-6 First XI football team photograph, a 1916 image of the Charterhouse school fire brigade, and the 1916 Gownboys House photograph. The house photograph features the seven seniors seated in the second row beside the housemaster, allowing us to narrow down possible identifications. With one boy in the row already previously identified, we compared the six other faces to those in the two other group photographs. One individual appears in all three, making this most likely Donald.

With a confirmed identification of William and a reasonably plausible identification of Donald, we compared both boys to the photos Hester should have been in. There was one girl who seemed to show a family resemblance, appearing in both the Barry House and Barry officers' photograph. This girl shares facial features with both William and Donald, with the same shaped nose and brow. We'd used an entirely unscientific method, but this being Hester would make sense. She fit well in a set with her brothers.

When we showed these images to some of Hester's relatives, we asked if they could identify the girl they thought most likely to be her. They weren't sure, but they did point to one individual in the image and profess their hope that it wasn't her, as she looked rather miserable. They had pointed right to the person we believed to be

Hester. After a little explanation of the similarities we saw between this girl and Hester's brothers, they had to admit they could see a family resemblance.

There is, of course, no conclusive proof here that we've found an image of Hester. It's a lot of guesswork, a lot of squinting at digitised images, and the following of several hunches. Most of us are fairly convinced that both the bridesmaid in the wedding photograph and the girl in the Wycombe Abbey photographs are, indeed, Hester, but it's impossible to get a confirmation. Still, they are as good as we've got for now. They've since been used in news segments and articles and no one has ever come forward to complain that, no, actually, that's not Hester Leggatt, that's their own grandmother. We still harbour a slight worry that one day that message will come and we'll be left with no decent quality images of her at all, and no further leads on where to look for one, but for now, we want to believe the girl in the photographs is Hester.

CHAPTER EIGHT

WELCOME TO THE BRITISH GOVERNMENT

WITH Hester's childhood and family tree established, we turned our attention to trying to track her career, in the hopes that we could conclusively prove she had been the Hester Leggatt working at MI5.

The Wycombe Abbey school records had allowed us to trace her to St James's Secretarial College, but from there, the trail went cold. If we couldn't go directly from one workplace to the next, we would have to find her some other way.

When exactly Hester finished her time at the Secretarial College is unclear, and we lose track of her for a few years in the early part of her career. In 1930, however, she was living in Earl's Court with her parents, so we knew we were still looking at London when it came to our search efforts.

Our next breakthrough came from the University of Reading archives, in a series comprising the papers of R.L. Mégroz. Rodolphe Louis Mégroz was an English writer and poet who served in the British Army during World War One. One of the books he wrote was entitled *The Three Sitwells; a biographical and critical study* (1927), concerning the lives of Edith, Osbert and Sacheverell Sitwell, a trio of siblings who excelled at poetry and writing.

Mégroz was close enough to the middle Sitwell sibling to send Osbert letters from 1925 to 1949, the replies to which formed their own subsection of the series held by the University of Reading. Two of these letters, one from 4th November 1933 and the other from 22nd January 1935, were written by Hester, on behalf of Osbert Sitwell, and signed in her now unmistakeable hand.

Exactly how and when Hester came to work as Osbert Sitwell's secretary is unclear, but it was a working relationship that spanned multiple years. In May 1935, he inscribed a copy of *Brighton* to her, a book he had co-authored with Margaret Barton, concerning the history of the eponymous city. The inscription reads 'For, Miss Hester Leggatt, in friendship, May 1935', the language of which is consistent with other books he gifted to his staff. A similar formulation of words is used in a copy inscribed to a Miss Noble, the housekeeper at the Sitwell family estate in Renishaw.

The discovery of the book was proof of how online traces can linger, with a Google search for Hester's name bringing up a webpage for a book that had been sold by Beaux Books, with the listing including the wording of the inscription.

When we started our research, an internet search for 'Hester Leggatt' didn't bring back all that many results, so going through them all wasn't too onerous. Now we're victims of our own success, with the results pages dominated by the identification of her and articles about our research. Despite it potentially burying any other chance mentions of Hester in the country's archives and catalogues, we're proud to have flooded the internet, rather inescapably, with her true identification, to make up for the years of misspelling and misremembering.

The *Brighton* inscription is not the only book dedicated to Hester that's been sold in recent years. Our searches also came back with a hit from a site belonging to the well-known auction house, Christie's. A lot of three books relating to Golden Cockerel Press had been sold in 2004, one of which was *The Journal of James Morrison, Boatswain of the Bounty*, a book published in 1935 and edited by Owen Rutter.

The copy was number 21 of 325 and had been presented to Hester, with the inscription reading 'For Hester from Owen with renewed thanks for the patience and care with which she copied the Journal. April 15, 1935.' From this inscription it seemed Hester had, at the same time as she'd been working for Sitwell, been taking on freelance work for Golden Cockerel Press, or perhaps for Owen Rutter directly.

Golden Cockerel Press originated as a private printing press and was in business from 1920 to 1961, focusing on handmade limited editions, explaining the rather small print run of the book Hester had worked on. The type would be hand-set and printed onto handmade paper, often accompanied with intricate original illustrations. Owen Rutter was one of a group of three men who bought the press in 1933, at which point it wasn't doing particularly well. It shifted from a private press to a publishing house, with Rutter's job being to solicit new books and work as editor on some of the projects.

The business was not doing a roaring trade. Most of the books published were losing money, with over half the copies of each book remaining unsold. The trio of men even considered buying a competitor press just so they could close it down and have a bigger share of the market. *The Journal of James Morrison, Boatswain of the Bounty* was certainly not a commercial success, and likely many copies of the book languished in storage. When World War Two began, however, interest in books increased and by 1943, almost all of the backlog of Golden Cockerel stock had been sold. Readers' desire for escapism had grown and constrained wartime production struggled to print enough new books to keep up, so a warehouse full of unsold volumes went from a problem to an opportunity.

With only 325 copies out there, *The Journal of James Morrison, Boatswain of the Bounty* proved itself not to be a particularly easy book to track down. The proximity of some of our researchers to London once again paid off, and a visit to the British Library was organised to view their copy. It features the detailed illustrations indicative of the press, as well as an introduction by Rutter, in which he discusses the process of turning James Morrison's volume into a published volume. He praises the work of 'Miss Hester Leggatt', who had prepared a copy of the manuscript under his supervision, thanking her for work 'which demanded great attention and accuracy'. Hester's name was not just in her own presentation copy, but in every copy of the book – even if that was only 325 bindings.

Rutter's book concerned the mutiny aboard the HMS Bounty on 28th April 1789, where crewmen took control of the ship and set their captain and 18 others adrift. In the same introduction in which he thanks Hester, Rutter also discusses his inability to locate an adequate amount of source material, recalling that 'when I appealed to Sir Basil Thomson, another authority on Bountiana, he told me that he too had searched for it in vain'.

Sir Basil Home Thomson, who had worked as Assistant Commissioner at Scotland Yard and Home Office Director of Intelligence, also wrote crime novels. One of these novels, published in 1937, was entitled 'The Milliner's Hat Mystery', and featured an interestingly familiar story of a dead body and a lot of forged paperwork. It is this story that was the direct inspiration for suggestion Number 28 in the Trout Memo, which posited that Hitler might be fooled by a corpse in uniform with documents in his pockets. It was this suggestion that eventually became Operation Mincemeat.

All of this research had taken us through Hester's life up to 1935. To fill in more gaps, we turned to the 1939 Register. This record provides a snapshot of the population on 29th September 1939, just after the outbreak of war. It was used to issue identity cards and ration books, as well as to organise conscription and to monitor the movement of people as a result of mobilisation and evacuation from cities threatened by air raids.

Hester is listed in the 1939 Register as living at flat 3A Wetherby Mansions, Earl's Court with her mother, and her occupation recorded as 'private secretary'. This is possibly the kind of response you might give if you were working on top secret MI5 business and you weren't sure whether you were allowed to be more specific, but considering Hester was able to tell Wycombe Abbey she'd worked for the War Office, this didn't quite feel right. With the war only a few weeks old by this point, it seemed more likely that Hester perhaps had not yet begun her work with MI5.

Sure enough, we also discovered a letter written by Maynard Hollingworth, the agent for the Sitwell's family estate, Renishaw. This letter was written to Hester and dated 18th January 1939. At this time, Hester was still the secretary to Osbert Sitwell, so it seems that the 'private secretary' position she had at the time of the 1939 Register, was indeed this position that she had maintained with Sitwell for at least six years.

It was the current Leggatt family who provided us with our next piece of information regarding her career. While they had no photographs of Hester (something complicated by the early death of her brother, William, so loss of contact with his side of the family), they did have a letter from the British Council that had been sent to Susan Leggatt, Hester's niece, after her death, and they were kind enough to send it on.

The letter was dated 14th August 1995, three weeks after Hester passed away, and was sent by the Acting Director of Corporate Personnel. It offered condolences on behalf of Hester's friends and colleagues at the British Council, stating that she was known to be calm and very confident, as well as hardworking. She had been very well liked by those who had worked with her and would be greatly missed by those who knew her. The British Council had a tradition of donating to charity in memory of staff who pass away, and they did so in Hester's memory to Samaritans, a suicide prevention charity, after being informed by her solicitor that it was a charity she had taken an interest in.

Thrilled to have a new lead, we reached out to the British Council in the hope of tracking down her personnel records. While they were quick to respond and as helpful as they could be, they were unable to provide us with much more information. Hester's personnel file had either been destroyed or lost during an office move. All that remained were her pension details, which were largely uninspiring. They did reveal that part of her pension had been paid by the Home Pension Scheme, issued by the North British and Mercantile Insurance Co. Ltd, from previous work before her time at the British Council, but the exact work was not specified.

They were also able to give us a rough idea of her time at the British Council. She began working there on the 7th of February 1946, at the age of 40, and first worked for the Home Division in Visitors, then in Education, followed by Budget and Control, and finally, by 1958, the Periodicals department. Hester dedicated a large amount of her life to the organisation.

The British Council's goals are to promote international cultural relationships, develop a wider knowledge of the English Language, and promote education both abroad and in the United Kingdom. It was created in the 1930s by Rex Leeper, a member of the UK Foreign Office, and was granted a Royal Charter in 1940 by King George VI.

Many of the international offices of the British Council had been closed in World War Two, but they had supported the British War effort by offering support to wartime refugees coming to England, as well as Allied service personnel who had been stationed here. During the 1950s, with the world recovering from two wars in quick succession, Hester would have been part of the setting up of two libraries in Pakistan, one in Lahore, and one in Karachi. This latter city, once in India, was where Hester herself had been born and seems to have spent her early years. One cannot help but wonder whether she had anything to do with the choice of location.

We had tracked down Hester before the war and after the war, but that still left the key period in the middle. All signs suggested that she had indeed been working at MI5 and getting involved with Operation Mincemeat, but we wanted indisputable evidence, and the best way to get that is always to go straight to the source.

It's quite hard to contact MI5. They don't provide a phone number for you to quickly get in touch with their records manager to voice a query. As frustrating as this was, it was also fairly understandable. The people in charge of the National Security Service undoubtedly have more important things to do than to answer questions about people who worked for them 70 years earlier. Letters were always a key part of this story anyway, so we sent one to MI5, politely asking for any information they might have on Hester Leggatt, including, if possible, confirmation of her employment, her job title, and the dates she had worked there.

Owing to the work MI5 do, they will only release information, even just confirmation of employment, once an individual is dead. Otherwise they risk putting retired employees and their families in harm's way. Dutifully, we also sent off Hester's death certificate. As hard as it was to contact MI5, it was surprisingly easy to order a copy of the certificate. You sign up to the General Register Office and then it takes 10 minutes and costs you £12.50. Somehow it seemed almost too easy, but we weren't about to complain.

The problem with Hester's death certificate was that it came with a few errors. Apparently never one to escape the constant misspelling of parts of her name, she is recorded as Hester Mary Murray Leggatt, when her first middle name was in fact May. This error reared its head a few times throughout her life, but never on quite so crucial a document.

Her place of birth is also down as England instead of Karachi, India. Both of these inconsistences threatened our attempts to verify her employment at MI5. We contemplated not mentioning them and hoping that perhaps they would go unnoticed, but this was MI5 we were dealing with and an eye for detail is probably something they value, so we explained each one and could only wait, hoping for the best.

By August 2023, the number of *Operation Mincemeat* fans in the Mincefluencer Discord had been growing steadily for a few months. Each performance of the show usually had at least one Discord member present to report back on any set malfunctions, line flubs, or dropped props, probably to the continual terror of the cast. People were making friends in this online space and then going on to meet in person at the show, and it seemed time to organise something bigger.

Fan performances of shows are nothing new. Musicals that appeal to younger audience demographics have increasingly been putting on events that encourage cosplay, singing along, and fan involvement. There weren't yet quite enough of us to take over the entire Fortune Theatre, but some organisation with the producers resulted in a large number of seats being made available for a group discount, and with that, planning for the first unofficial Mincefluencer fan event began in earnest.

The trip became known as Operation Interesting Man, an obscure reference to a character in the show that never even made it into the final Southwark Playhouse run. In a scene set at MI5 outside Colonel Bevan's office, four characters discuss the plans they're going to present to the big boss. At first, the line up on stage included everyone except Zoë Roberts, who would appear in comedy disguise glasses as a kind of assistant to welcome Montagu in to give his pitch. After Montagu remarked that the assistant was an 'interesting man', Zoë entered the stage as James Bond author Ian Fleming and Natasha Hodgson exited.

Then the only one off stage, Natasha was the only person able to play the assistant for his next entrance. She donned the same glasses with attached plastic nose and entered to welcome in the rest of the men to give their pitches. When her identity was questioned, she proclaimed to be the 'same man, the same interesting man'.

It was a fairly ludicrous moment in the show that was later rendered obsolete by some reorganising of entrances and exits in the scene, but it was sorely missed by the fans who had seen it, so it became the theme of the planning. The existence of an emoji that matched the look of the character's novelty glasses cemented the naming decision and the little yellow face was adopted by fans on social media in the run up to the event.

Roughly 80 fans turned up to the evening performance of the show that night for Operation Interesting Man, many of them in cosplay. The main costumes of the show are shirts and suit trousers, which arguably makes cosplaying (the practice of a person making and wearing a costume from a favourite piece of media) fairly easy. For some this meant simply sourcing a white shirt and dark trousers, for others it meant intense searches to match exact patterns on shirt fabrics and stripes on suspender elastic.

There were handsewn costumes and thrifted costumes,

with Vinted and Depop likely being stripped of suit trousers. Some fans opted to recreate specific props or accessories, digging deep into the show's lyrics to mine them for in-jokes and tiny references that they turned into outfits. The pre-show line-up of costumes in the alleyway next to the Fortune Theatre perfectly represented the Mincefluencers: bizarre, detail-orientated, niche, and dedicated.

The crowd of clearly enthusiastic fans posed a slight concern for security at the venue, but after a heartfelt promise not to disturb any regular audience members, we filed into the theatre to watch a very high-energy show.

Other than the widespread confusion from the uniniti-ated at being faced with dozens of people dressed as if it was the 1940s, a plethora of sequins and rhinestones, and more than one person dressed as a flamingo, it was all kept very civil. A few unsuspecting victims were even persuaded to join the ranks by the end of the evening, bol-stering the Discord server numbers even further. As far as we know, there was not one single complaint.

After the show came to an end, we were invited to wait in the stalls for everyone else to leave the auditorium so a photograph could be taken of our fully-assembled numbers.

During the show, one member of the #FindingHester team had received a message saying there was a seemingly important letter waiting for them at home. A plain white envelope marked 'Private & Confidential'. From the description given, it matched a previous MI5 letter that had asked for a copy of Hester's death certificate.

Frantic messages asking for the envelope to be opened weren't answered quickly enough, so the conversation was escalated to a phone call. As the rest of the group gathered in front of the stage for the photograph, one researcher paced at the back of the stalls as the letter was read out to them.

The first paragraph laid out the rules MI5 adheres to when disclosing information, so the first few minutes of the call were disheartening. Maybe we'd missed some piece of information we should have provided. Maybe they wouldn't tell us because we weren't family. Maybe the incorrect middle name and place of birth on the death certificate meant they couldn't confirm their identity. When dealing with the country's Security Service, the devil could easily be in the details.

In the next paragraph, however, the tone completely changes. Yes, Hester May Murray Leggatt had worked at MI5 from 3rd June 1940 to 31st July 1945. She was the 'Hester Leggett' Jean Leslie identified as working on Operation Mincemeat.

It was finally concrete information that all of our research had not been for nothing. There couldn't have been a better moment to receive the news. It was announced to the assembled crowd, including many of the researchers, in the theatre where Hester was being brought to life eight times a week. The majority of Mincefluencers might not have been directly involved in the research, but they all supported the efforts and the news was incredibly welcomed, received with cheers, applause, and even some tears.

We could have stopped there. We had the confirmation that we'd truly found Hester and likely no one would have judged us for considering that a fitting conclusion to the project, but we weren't done. There were still open avenues of research, and a lot more people were about to hear the name Hester Leggatt – correct spelling and all.

ADDITIONAL RESEARCH: FINDING AVERIL

GREG CALLUS

THROUGHOUT the #FindingHester project, we were keeping an eye out for potential colleagues or friends of Hester – especially if, like Jean, they were younger than her by a significant margin – in the hope of tracing some-one who knew her and was still alive. One tangent was particularly enticing.

In Ewen Montagu's *The Man Who Never Was Man Who Never Was*, published in 1953, he had said the following about the commissioning of the letters by 'Pam':

None of us had felt up to writing the letters – after all, ours was not the feminine point of view – and it was a bit difficult to ask a girl if she could write a first-rate paeon of love. So we asked a girl working in one of the offices whether she could get some girl to do it. She took on the job but never would tell us the name of the girl who produced the magnificent letters that Major Martin was to carry with him.

Everything Montagu says in *The Man Who Never Was Man Who Never Was* needs to be taken with a full tablespoon of salt, but on this account, Montagu and Cholmondeley asked Woman A (whose identity they obviously knew) to get Woman B (whom they did not know) to produce the letters. We, at least, now know Woman B to be Hester Leggatt.

Woman A returns later on in *The Man Who Never Was Man Who Never Was* with the pseudonym 'Jill', in a rather curious final act of preparation. One of the ways in which Operation Mincemeat sought to convince the recipients of Major Martin's body that he had travelled by aircraft was by having him discovered with used ticket stubs to a West End show from just a day or so earlier. The logic, which was duly followed in the official reports in Spain, was that if he had seen the show (which was three days after HMS Seraph had set sail on 19 April 1943) the only way he could have subsequently reached Huelva so quickly was by travelling by air, thus supporting the crash-landing theory.

To effect this deception, four tickets were bought to Sid Fields' new show *Strike a New Note* at the Prince of Wales Theatre for the evening of Thursday 22nd April 1943, a variety show starring a young Eric Morecambe and Ernie

Wise. Two of the tickets were pristine, but two had their stubs torn-off, for inclusion amongst the pocket-litter in Major Martin's wallet.

However, once HMS Seraph had set sail, were still two untouched and two 'used' stubless tickets for the show. Never ones to miss an opportunity, Montagu and Cholmondeley enjoyed a night out which was informally christened 'Bill Martin's Farewell Party'. They managed to persuade the staff at the theatre that the missing stubs were just the consequence of a practical joke (which was not strictly untrue). Accordingly, four people attended the show: Montagu took Jean Leslie as his 'date'; Cholmondeley took as his date the woman whom *The Man Who Never Was Man Who Never Was* calls 'Jill, the girl who had arranged for the writing of the love letters.'

After the theatre, the four of them – Montagu, Cholmondeley, Jean and 'Jill' – went for dinner at the Gargoyle Club. This was a notorious private members club on the corner of Dean Street and Meade Street in Soho (and in the musical of *Operation Mincemeat* is depicted as being the place that Monty and Charlie meet Ivor during the song *Just For Tonight*).

We have a specific detail of this dinner from *The Man Who Never Was Man Who Never Was*. First, Montagu says that he offered the ladies the more comfortable banquette to sit on, so he and Cholmondeley would take the less-comfortable chairs. This causes 'Jill' to make the humorous comment 'Considering Bill and Pam are engaged, they are the least affectionate couple I know. They don't even want to sit together at his farewell party before he goes abroad.' Apparently, this remark led to a rather suggestive reply from Montagu, which caused some consternation at a nearby table, who flounce off to have a dance. But what is important is that Montagu, as the author of *The Man Who Never Was Man Who Never Was* attributes this comment made in his presence to 'Jill', the 'girl who had arranged the writing of the love letters.'

Ben Macintyre's 2010 book *Operation Mincemeat* also carries this same tale, beginning his Chapter 14 with the 'Bill Martin Farewell Party'. But what Macintyre adds to *The Man Who Never Was Man Who Never Was* is the two names that were given to him by Jean Leslie when he interviewed her towards the end of her life. This entire project, and indeed this book, begins with Jean telling Macintyre about 'Hester Leggett'. But Jean also told Macintyre the identity of 'Jill' with whom she had attended the 'Farewell Party' at the theatre and Gargoyle Club. The name which Jean gave Macintyre was 'Avril Gordon'.

Macintyre writes up the 'Farewell Party' saying 'Charles Cholmondeley's date for the evening was Avril Gordon, another young secretary in the office who had helped Hester Leggett compose "Pam's" letters,' and goes on to attribute 'Jill's' comments about Bill and Pam being the 'least affectionate couple' to this 'Avril Gordon.' As well as getting Jill's real name, we are told she is 'young'. This tracks with Jean being just 19 at the date of the Farewell Party, and Cholmondeley would only have been 26 (and so his 'date' would no doubt have been younger).

Accordingly, we were keen to look for 'Avril Gordon' who (assuming she was between the ages of 18 and 26 at the time of the 'Farewell Party') might still be alive and in her late 90s as of the summer of 2023.

The problem, as with Hester 'Leggett', was that no such 'Avril Gordon' appeared to have been born between 1925 and 1931 anywhere near London. There was no sign of her in the 1939 Register, or in addresses in electoral registers in the surrounding decades. Certain candidates based on newspaper reports were either entirely associated with other cities, like Belfast or Glasgow, or did not entirely fit for other reasons, like a nurse in Cheltenham with the same name who had an illegitimate child early on in World War Two.

The problem, like with 'Leggett,' appeared to be the problem of a spelling error creeping in during the course of Jean giving the name to Macintyre. How confident could we be in Jean's memory of the spelling of a colleague's name six-and-a-half decades later? Might it not be Avril but instead Averil, Averill, or Averell? Was the surname really Gordon, not Cordon – there were several people called 'Cordon' at one wedding attended by Hester's relatives. Full-scale trawls of genealogy websites, newspaper archives and web searches didn't render any suitable candidates, even on these anticipated variants.

We slightly gave up on finding Avril.

But on 2nd August 2023, three researchers went to the archives of the Imperial War Museum in South London. The IWM holds three full boxes of Montagu's private papers, and a wealth of primary materials and records, which convey information that could never be found anywhere else. Amongst other documents which scratched our investigative itches, it identified every person in the Room 17M photograph (as well as confirming that Room 17M had very little to do with Operation Mincemeat, which was run by Section B1A of MI5 under the direction of Montagu and Cholmondeley). It gave us definitive confirmation of our longstanding suspicions that Hester (a stalwart of B1A) and Jean (one of the 'beavers' in Section B1B) were not in the Room 17M photograph at all.

Less obviously exciting than the primary documents were the masses of newspapers and other press clippings kept by Montagu. Almost all of them concerned two topics: (1) matters relating to the story of Operation Mincemeat (both contemporaneous accounts of the invasion of Sicily, and later press coverage of *The Man Who Never Was Man Who Never Was* in book and film format); and (2) the awful plight of the Jewish people in mainland Europe and the discovery of the details of the Holocaust perpetrated upon them. These newspapers were a portal into the mind of Montagu, and the things that he cared about enough to archive, but they told us little we didn't already know about Operation Mincemeat itself.

One researcher, however, has a very sharp eye. She found two things that day of monumental importance to our project. The first was a memo to Montagu dated 27th July 1945 concerning the Operation Mincemeat papers. It was signed 'HL' in a hand which seemed identical to the hand-writing samples of Hester that we had obtained from the R.L. Mégroz archives at the University of Reading. Importantly, it confirmed that this HL had been in Section B1A of MI5, the unit which Montagu's concluding operational memo of 27th April 1943 confirmed was primarily responsible for the execution of Operation Mincemeat: 'From then on the operation was devised and all preparations made by Lt Commander Montagu with the assistance of Flight Lieutenant Cholmondeley and some of the staff of B.1.A Section of MI5.'

But the researcher also spotted an anomaly: a copy of *The Star* newspaper from 26th June 1945 which appeared to contain nothing about either Operation Mincemeat or the plight of the Jewish people in mainland Europe. There was no obvious reason why Montagu had kept this newspaper in his Operation Mincemeat papers at all. Until you looked at pages 4 and 5.

The middle of the double-page had a column of photographs under the heading 'Star News Reel', and the first entry says 'A Village Wedding'. The photograph depicts a bride arm-in-arm with a man dressed in military uniform, processing through crowds of children on each side. The photograph caption says 'The children of Burch, Suffolk, ran from school to the church and formed a spontaneous guard of honour for Lieut. David Milln and his bride, Miss Averil Gurdon, daughter of Major-Gen. and Mrs Gurdon, of Burch House, Suffolk.'

This incredible spot of a tiny detail in a photograph caption was of immediate and obvious relevance: Jean had told Macintyre that 'Jill' was 'Avril Gordon', but that could easily be elided with 'Averil Gurdon'. So the task became to discover what we could about Averil Gurdon.

Understandably for a person who shed her maiden name at the age of 21 (and may have been working at MI5 for her years of adulthood before her wedding), there wasn't much in the press about Averil Gurdon. She had been a bridesmaid in Sevenoaks, Kent, at the age of six, and was featured in *Country Life* magazine in 1944 as one of their 'girls in pearls'. She certainly fit the profile of a woman who worked at MI5 during the war, being the daughter of a Major-General in the British Army.

A proper search for Averil Gurdon on genealogy websites confirmed her age and lineage: the daughter of Major-General Edward Temple Leigh Gurdon CB, CBE, MC (known as Temple Gurdon). She was born on 17th April

1924, and so her 19th birthday was the Saturday just before the Thursday 'Farewell Party' at the Gargoyle Club.

Unless MI5 employed actual children during World War Two, she had been working at MI5 less than a year at the time the 'Pam' letters were commissioned through her. If Montagu's telling was correct, he asked Averil to find someone to write them, and Averil was responsible for choosing Hester (who, at 37, must have seemed much more experienced to an 18-year-old) from amongst the women in Section B1A. At least if *The Man Who Never Was Man Who Never Was* is to be believed, Montagu never knew the author was Hester, but knew of Averil, such to invite her to the farewell party and to remember her sufficiently fondly to have kept a newspaper report of her wedding.

One curiosity for historical research stemming from a West End musical is that Averil had a brother, Adam Gurdon, who followed his father into the military as a commander in the Black Watch. Adam's daughter Madeleine – who is Averil's niece – is married to none other than the composer Andrew Lloyd-Webber.

What was still missing was confirmation that our hunch – 'Averil Gurdon' being 'Avril Gordon' – was in fact correct. This confirmation came in two parts. The first was a very simple Google search under what we knew to be her married name 'Averil Milln'. That rendered only two results: a planning application, and a link on the IMDB (Internet Movie DataBase) website.

IMDB lists all cast and crew members in film and television series. It does so largely (but not exclusively) by reference to the credits that roll at the end of a programme or movie. Most people on IMDB are actors or other professionals involved in the making of TV or film. But the credits at the end of a programme also contain other participants and non-participants.

Averil Milln has only one credit on IMDB, under the credit heading of 'the BBC wishes to thank'. The credit is for a single episode of a long-running BBC television historical documentary series called *Timewatch*. The episode dates from 1999, which was the 18th series of the show which had premiered in 1982, and was the ninth episode in that series. The title of the episode: *The Spies Who Fooled Hitler: MI5 at War.*

The episode isn't (as might have been thought) primarily about Operation Mincemeat. Instead, it is an account of the Double Cross programme, which was the main focus of Section B1A in MI5 (who also ran Operation Mincemeat). Double Cross turned almost all Axis spies sent to the UK into double-agents, so that misinformation could be sent back to the Nazis.

The featured and named contributors in the credits include Peggy Harmer (credited as being a Secretary in Section B1A specifically) and Ronnie Reed (who was the 'face' of Major Martin on the forged identity card).

Although the episode isn't about Operation Mincemeat,

there could be only one rational explanation for a then 75-year-old Averil Milln to be thanked by the makers of a BBC documentary episode looking at Section B1A during World War Two, and that is because she was working in Section B1A during World War Two, prior to her marriage.

This development gave us the necessary degree of confidence to do what we did sparingly: contacting living relatives of people we were researching to see if they could corroborate our enquiries. In the case of Averil Milln, there was a public record that she had died almost 20 years earlier, but that she had living children. Shrewd use of genealogy websites allowed us to identify one of those children as Dr Phillip Milln, a Consultant Psychiatrist. He appeared to have a private practice based in the South of England, and so we called them to ask to speak to him. We were told that he had retired from practise, and so we drafted an email to be passed onto him.

Dr Milln contacted us very shortly afterwards. In summary, he was well aware that his late mother had been in MI5 during World War Two, but had not been specifically aware of any role she had in Operation Mincemeat (although he was familiar with it from the books and films). One particular act of generosity by Dr Phillip Milln was to email me photographs of Averil's 1943 appointments diary, with some examples of her handwriting. We talked about the role we understood that his mother had played in the 'Pam' letters.

He told me that she had described her time in MI5 as extraordinarily good fun – that to the young women with whom she worked, the war, as experienced from MI5 in London, was exciting and thrilling, and led to life-long friendships. He told me one particularly close friend of Averil Gurdon's (as she then was) for the remainder of her life was Peggy Harmer (born Margaret Gordon Phillips, which may explain Jean misspeaking to Ben Macintyre to say Averil's surname was 'Gordon' not 'Gurdon').

Peggy, like Averil, was the daughter of a Major-General in the British Army, Major-General Sir Leslie Gordon Phillips KBE CB MC. She was a fellow Section B1A secretary who married MI5 officer Christopher Harmer on Saturday 6th March 1943, a wedding we know Hester attended and who had contributed on-the-record to the 1999 episode of BBC's *Timewatch* in which Averil Milln (as she then was) was thanked.

This book, and this project, was always primarily about 'Finding Hester'. But if the musical has a message to live by, it is that those who work and contribute are often owed credit that history fails to give them. Averil Gurdon is one of those: a secretary in Section B1A of MI5 who did great and important work, and was a key link in the chain that led to Hester Leggatt writing the 'Pam' letters for Operation Mincemeat. In addition to #FindingHester, it has been our privilege to also #FindAveril.

CHAPTER NINE

FOR HESTER, WHO SERVED HER NATION

THROUGHOUT our research of Hester, the team behind the *Operation Mincemeat* musical had been hugely encouraging and supportive. From the first tweet that posited the potential identification of Hester as a Leggatt rather than a Leggett, the writers and cast were as invested in the research project as we were. They followed updates on Twitter and would be filled in on major developments at stage door after the show.

For Jak Malone, it was all a little overwhelming at first. We were only able to do our research because we knew of Hester's existence and had been moved to find out more about her, and it was Jak's performance of her in the show that had driven that interest. Without his nuanced, stern but soft, and tragic but hopeful portrayal, there would be no #FindingHester project. The magnitude of returning someone's identity to them because of his role meant he held the entire thing at arm's length until he had fully processed it.

But as we learnt more and more about Hester and found her living relatives, there was really no escaping what we were discovering. It was a topic frequently brought up in cast interviews and Q&As, where they were kind enough to say nice things about us and our research efforts. Any concerns about our sanity or the overabundance of free time we seemed to have were politely left unsaid.

While keeping up with our research, Jak even realised that he had a strange connection to Hester of his own. Thanks mostly to electoral rolls, we were able to curate a list of almost every address Hester had lived at, most of which were in London. Having just adopted an Italian greyhound puppy named Dracula, who himself is an icon in the Mincemeat community, Jak's girlfriend had arranged to pick up some items for him from someone who no longer needed them. The house she went to was one Hester had lived at. The coincidences continued, mundane but also weird and exciting all the same.

The merchandise stalls at the Fortune Theatre sell two programmes: a smaller booklet that features their vivid yellow and black artwork that hides a stylised image of Hitler's hair and moustache; and a larger brochure that shares its cover design with a prop file from the show, a large red cross from corner to corner, on a beige background. The pattern itself comes from a real Operation Mincemeat file in The National Archives.

Hester's name was obviously wrong in both of these programmes, considering that was all anyone knew when they were initially being printed at the start of the West End run. The larger volume took the fiction a step further. There was a page dedicated to each character, containing the real details of their lives and photographs of them. With no information available for Hester, her date of birth was down as '5th April 1894', to fit with the narrative the show had given Hester of loving and losing a soldier in World War One, and her date of death was simply 'unknown'. There was no photograph to add, of course, so one of the production shots of Jak as Hester was used instead.

At the end of August 2023, these programmes went to another printing and quiet alterations were made. Hester's name was corrected in the yellow programme and online, but the brochure took the changes one step further. They couldn't entirely remove the initial information from the page, because the earlier date of birth was key to the Hester they had created, but they did the next best thing. The page now came with edits, printed to look like someone had gone in with a pen to correct the historical record. Hester's incorrect surname, date of birth and date of death were crossed out, but still legible, and the real details of her life were filled in beside them.

Under the photo of Jak was a list of the names of the #FindingHester team, with the note 'with thanks to the team of researchers who unearthed Hester's identity and set these records straight'. Beside it was a QR code that took anyone who scanned it to the Google Doc we had been keeping updated with the bulk of our research. Paper clipped to the page in every copy of the brochure was an 'urgent memo' from SpitLip:

We were captivated by the mystery of Hester Leggatt from the moment we came across her. This austere, frightening woman with a soul full of romance: who could both terrify the typing pool and pour her heart into a love letter. But try as we might, we couldn't unearth the details of her life. They were simply not important enough to those in charge and – with a musical to write – other matters gradually became more pressing. We did what we could with the beautiful fragments we had. The real identity of Hester Leggatt fell, once again, into the background.

That might have been the end of the story, were it not for our show's community. Where we failed, they had the spark of an idea. Where we let the facts fall back into the shadows, they rolled up their sleeves and said "let's go." They took to archives, to libraries, to biographers, to MI5 itself, they worked together, this merry, passionate band, determined that this woman would get the place in history she deserved. And they did it. They found her.

FOR HESTER, WHO SERVED HER NATION

Hester May Murray Leggatt (1905-1995)

They went on this quest out of love, out of determination, of the simple desire to do something useful, together. We cannot imagine a more appropriate legacy for this story – and for Hester herself – than this.

Thank you, agents. The next musical really ought to be about you x

It is safe to say that more than one of us shed tears when we read this message in the theatre, passing along the advice that, even if you'd already bought a brochure before, you needed to buy another one. If it was a ploy to double the programme sales, it was effective, but the respect and appreciation felt sincere. The subtitle on the cover of the *Operation Mincemeat* brochure is 'The Mission Behind the Musical', and it felt like we'd become a part of that, somehow.

It was an absolute delight to see Hester's name spelt correctly in the programmes and online, and equally to see the Leggatts thanked in the back of the brochure alongside the Montagus and the Bevans. A piece of the puzzle, so long-lost it was gathering dust in the corner, had been restored. This was one of the things we'd wanted from the beginning, but we were about to see Hester's name spread far more broadly.

We had never been particularly quiet about our research efforts, often overflowing with enthusiasm to share the new information we'd gathered, so eventually people outside of the *Operation Mincemeat* bubble began to take notice. One of our number had written an article in the *Independent* as early as July, with theatre news outlets like *WhatsOnStage* starting to take notice in August. When we hit September, *Operation Mincemeat: The True Spy Story That Changed the Course of World War Two* author Ben Macintyre wrote an article in *The Times* about our MI5 confirmation, including the school picture we'd identified to most likely be Hester. Like proud parents collecting their child's achievements, many of us bought copies of the paper just to save the article. Jak Malone had once cited his feeling of protection over Hester, like he was responsible for carrying her banner, and now we felt it too. To see Hester's story told felt like our biggest accomplishment, but it didn't stop there.

BroadwayWorldUK and *The Stage* joined in, meaning every major UK theatre news outlet had featured the #FindingHester story. Even if one article did mistakenly refer to one of the team as an employee of MI5, which is as close as she's ever going to get to being a secret agent so she's not about to complain.

The next big event in the #FindingHester calendar would take place in December of that year. The researchers were invited to an event at the Fortune Theatre, where a plaque was to be unveiled.

In Act Two of *Operation Mincemeat*, Hester and Jean sing

Useful, a song in which they imagine the acclaim they might get after the war. At first, it's Jean who pictures medals, and personal thanks from Winston Churchill and King George VI. Hester lets her have her dream but tries to stay grounded, before Jean convinces her to imagine a statue in her honour. Hester rejects the notion, but admits to liking the idea of 'perhaps just a small plaque.' She wants something 'tasteful and small', but Jean pushes her further, until she envisions something gold and dazzling, remembering her with the inscription 'For Hester, who served her nation.'

The song ends with Hester and Jean both acknowledging the fact that they were unlikely to get any recognition at all, and certainly not statues or plaques, and that they'd have to be content with knowing they'd made themselves useful. As we got further into our research, we tentatively started to explore ways to give Hester the memorial she deserved. One option we looked into was an English Heritage blue plaque, a scheme first started in 1866 that records links between important historic figures and present buildings. They didn't think Hester qualified.

We then turned to the idea of a bench in a London park, considering the lyric in *Useful* that sees Hester imagining her plaque in 'a grand royal park', but these benches were both prohibitively expensive and temporary. Besides, the link to a royal park was something specific to SpitLip's Hester, not the real Hester we had uncovered.

The lobby of the Fortune Theatre is tiny. Actually, the same can be said of the entire front of house space. There is an oft-repeated story that the entire footprint of the building, including the stage and auditorium, the bars, the toilets, and the dressing rooms, can fit on just the stage of the 2,000-seat Theatre Royal Drury Lane over the road. The Fortune is a rabbit warren of staircases and bars the size of generous cupboards. On 11th December 2023, as many people were packed into the theatre's lobby as possible. The show's cast and writers were there, as were a line of media cameras, members of the Leggatt family, the #FindingHester researchers, and a gathering of Mincefluencers, who, considering the scenes outside of everyone struggling, and failing, to fit onto the pavement, ought to take the collective noun name 'a chaos of Mincefluencers'.

On the back wall of the lobby, right next to the box office and directly facing everyone who enters the theatre, was a set of curtains. They were, of course, appropriately Mincemeat yellow and embroidered with a pair of roses, as mentioned in Hester's big song *Dear Bill*.

After a slight struggle to quiet the assembled numbers, SpitLip launched into an unveiling ceremony. Despite Natasha Hodgson's promise to try not to cry, she made it one sentence into the first speech of the night before she started choking up:

'Art doesn't change things, but it changes the people

who change things, and we've been thinking about just how incredible it is that a song in a musical could inspire a group of brilliant, amazing people to embark on a real life mission, to create a community, to travel the country, to dive in archives and go through newspapers, and make it all the way to the files of MI5 itself, in order to right a historical wrong and to give an amazing woman a place in her story.'

Both she and David Cumming went on to cite our research as proof of the value of art, and the power of creativity to inspire people and to fight injustice. We stand by their message wholeheartedly, but while they put the spotlight on us, it deserves to be turned back on them. Without SpitLip's silly little musical, none of this would have happened. No one would ever know who Hester really was, and the misspelling of her name and loss of her story would only have continued.

Hester is no longer around to speak for herself, of course, but to hear one of her great nephews continu-ing the speeches by saying 'Hester herself would be very gratified to see everything that's going on here,' felt like the biggest compliment we could have been awarded. Whether she would have wanted a plaque was anyone's guess, and whether she would have liked the musical at all is also up for debate, but we felt that, with her family's approval, we had done her proud.

Jak Malone also fought off tears as he reiterated his

belief that playing Hester is the biggest honour of his life so far, commending 'the fully realised, wonderful woman' we had uncovered. He wasn't alone in his emotion, with many in the audience equally moved by both the words being said and the people who had assembled. For the researchers, it had been six months since we'd started looking into Hester. With so much of that work based online, it was the first time some of us had ever met each other in person, but we'd always been united across the country in one goal.

With the conclusion of the speeches, a gold plaque was unveiled.

It read 'FOR HESTER, WHO SERVED HER NATION', and then records her correct full name and dates of existence, before rightly acknowledging her as 'a vital contributor of MI5's Operation Mincemeat (1943).' We expected this commemoration of Hester, but what we didn't expect was the rest of the text on the plaque.

Underneath, it read:

The Operation Mincemeat musical team would like to thank the researchers who unearthed her identity

It then listed the names of the entire #FindingHester team. Hester had finally received her plaque, but we had one too. It was an extraordinary moment, to be recognised so centrally in the continuation of Hester's story.

In the time between the unveiling of the plaque and

the theatre opening for the show that night, a large group of us filed into a Pret A Manger in Covent Garden for some food. They really weren't thrilled to see a group of 15 people walk in when they were winding down for the night, but we were desperate to get out of the cold December air. After promising that we wouldn't leave a mess in an area of seating they already wanted to close off, we gathered round a large table and, with small groups crowded around a number of phones, we watched the news that night. Hester was there, the story broadcast to the nation on both BBC News and Sky News. The plaque and her picture were shown, and we felt hugely grateful that her story had been recognised as important by people outside of our group. She was worth talking about on the Six O'Clock News.

It's probably not even worth saying that we cried, because of course we did. Even watching the news articles back on YouTube while writing this book, they still bring tears to the eyes. During that night's performance of the show, *Useful* probably matched *Dear Bill* for the number of tears shed. We'd proved the fictional Hester wrong. As she sung how no one would see the work she did, we knew everyone would see it. It was already an emotional moment in the show, with Hester and Jean finally reconciling their differences to express their mutual respect for one another and acknowledge they're in the same position. Now it would carry an additional new meaning for all of us.

Hester's name had not only been corrected, but her story had been shared with more people than we ever imagined. In the following days, we would be invited onto radio shows to talk about the research and the plaque, delighted but ever-stunned that a few tweets had snowballed into this.

If this had been the end of the story, it would have felt fitting. We found Hester and then we'd told the world, from a larger platform that we had ever envisaged. Perhaps, however, Hester wasn't quite done finding us, because we were soon to receive another piece of the puzzle.

ADDITIONAL RESEARCH: FINDING WATKINS

CLAUDIA CAPLAN WOLFF

The investigation into Hester set off a frenzy of research but, maybe because I'm an American, I noticed that there was no #find-Willie channel on the Discord server. I requested that one be created and began my research, along with others interested in his story.

Willie Watkins is also portrayed in the original *Operation Mincemeat* cast by Jak Malone. Quite the opposite of Malone's controlled and proper Hester, Watkins is a loud, enthusiastic American pilot. In fact, Malone characterises his portrayal as 'larger than life' and likens Willie Watkins to the blustering Warner Brothers cartoon character, Foghorn Leghorn. Malone also refers to Willie's 'job' in the show as being a 'big inconvenience' and in a recent interview he shared that originally there had been an entire scene with Watkins participating in – and almost scuttling – the autopsy. Though this scene was cut from the final script, it did inform how he thought about the character.

He was also influenced by going to drama school with quite a few Americans and realising he was more British than he thought, particularly when it came to 'stiff upper lip-ness.' To portray an American he had to acknowledge that the stereotypes and clichés are often an accurate representation of the differences between being British and being American.

It is undoubtedly inconvenient that Watkins happens to ditch his plane on the beach in Huelva shortly before Major William Martin is scheduled to make an appearance in the same spot. He provides comic relief but also tension at a pivotal moment when Montagu, Cholmondeley and everyone at MI5 are waiting to see if William Martin will indeed show up and fool the Nazis. As Jean Leslie and Cholmondeley sing in *The Ballad of Willie Watkins*, 'the Germans will be disbelieving, when they hear two pilots crashed in neutral Spain.' By contrast, when Willie sings, he harmonises with Natasha Hodgson as Ewen Montagu as there is some kinship between the larger-than-life quality of both characters, even though they are on a divided stage representing both Huelva and London.

Playing the only American character in the show, Malone says that he can tell when there are Americans in the audience, as there frequently are. Haselden's line, 'It's worse than that, he's an American' elicits a particular response. Malone put it this way, 'It pokes on those old wartime rivalries.' As one of those Americans in the audience, his over-the-top portrayal of a Yank who literally crashes the plot, his 'Jeez Louise' exclamations and belting musical style made me wonder if there had indeed been a real Willie Watkins.

To answer that question, I referred back to Ben Macintyre's *Operation Mincemeat* and, sure enough, there he was, recorded as crash-landing an American P-39 Airacobra plane in a field in Punta Umbria just three days before MI5's body was brought ashore. The pilot identified was 26-year-old Watkins from Corpus Christi, Texas. He had departed from North Africa headed for Portugal, but had crashed when his plane ran out of fuel.

Macintyre goes on to write about Watkins's presence at the autopsy of William Martin as a result of a request from the Spanish Army lieutenant Pascual de Pobil, who thought the two incidents of Allied planes crashing might somehow be related.

There was a real Willie Watkins, and I was determined to find him. In many ways, when it came to finding the real person behind the name, there was a bigger identification problem than that posed by the misspelling of Hester's last name. The last name Watkins might just as well have been Smith or Jones considering its ubiquity in the United States. Starting with U.S. World War Two draft and induction records, the number of William/Willard/Willis/Wilbert Watkins was overwhelming. There were hundreds, if not thousands. And that didn't even take into account a person who might have acquired the moniker 'Willie' as a result of a middle name or some family nick-naming quirk. The only other hints were 'Corpus Christi, Texas' and Willie's age at the time of the accident – 26.

As it turned out, while one of these pieces of information was helpful, the other was entirely wrong.

The fact that Willie was an aviator narrowed the field. In fact, one of the most important things in Macintyre's account was the type of aircraft Watkins was flying. The P-39 Airacobra was flown by very few units in the World War Two United States Army Air Corps (the precursor to the Air Force). And while it was the plane of choice for the African-American Tuskegee Airmen, this didn't seem like a place to look for Willie. It seemed more likely that he would be with one of the major P-39 operators, including the 81st and 350th Fighter Groups, both flying maritime patrol missions from North Africa and on through Italy. The timing was particularly plausible for the 81st Fighter Group which had been constituted on 31st January 1942, trained in England, and arrived in North Africa between late December 1942 and early February 1943. Flying out of North Africa on reconnaissance seemed a reasonable way to crash land in Huelva, Spain, and the timing was right, as William Martin's body was found on 30th April 1943.

The Army Air Corps records available online included Missing Air Crew Men information, but there were two problems. One, the records had been uploaded in the form of facsimile index cards with only a name. They hadn't been digitised and weren't searchable. Two, we had no middle name for Willie Watkins and so there was the ongoing Wilbur/ Wilfred/etc. problem, with no way to pinpoint our Willie Watkins.

One of the other researchers working on Willie found an index card with a record of an Oak Leaf Cluster Air Medal Decoration for a William Powell Watkins. The citation mentioned Northwest Africa and the date was 10th April 1943. This seemed promising, particularly as William Powell Watkins was an aviator from Galveston, Texas, but a newspaper story from 'Allied Headquarters in North Africa' dashed those hopes. William Powell Watkins was a navigator flying in a bomber, not a fighter pilot. Crucially, he had died on 6th April 1943, more than three weeks before William Martin's body washed up in Huelva.

Another clue came from an obituary in the *San Antonio Express-News* for Air Force Brigadier General Tarleton Watkins, who died on 12th December 2009. The obituary mentioned that, 'He lost three brothers in World War Two; William and Robert, in action in Italy and at sea respectively and the youngest, Woodruff, in a flight training accident.' It was a long shot, but maybe General Watkins's brother William was Operation Mincemeat's Willie Watkins.

So, finding the real Willie Watkins started in earnest with the bright orange draft card of a 21-year-old student from the University of Virginia. The card stated his name as William Anderson Watkins, his age as 21 and his place of birth as Corpus Christi, Texas.

Comparing the draft card to General Tarleton Watkins's obituary provided the necessary link. General Watkins's obituary says that his father was Colonel Dudley Warren Watkins. William Anderson Watkins's draft card identifies his father as Major D.W. Watkins. Armed with that information and with the help of newspapers.com, I dug into news stories from World War Two that mentioned Tarleton Watkins (a far easier name to find) or William Anderson Watkins, to see if I could somehow connect him to the downed pilot in Huelva.

On a parallel track, I saw that Macintyre had footnoted a book written in Spanish about Operation Mincemeat in his explanation of the autopsy. The book Macintyre cited was *Espías y Neutrales: Huelva en la Guerra Mundial* by Jesús Copeiro del Villar. With a bit of research, I discovered that Señor Copeiro del Villar and a co-author, Enrique Nielsen, had written a more recent book: *William Martin: Crónica de la operación Carne Picada*. Or, in English, the story of Operation Mincemeat. Luckily, I had a local connection. My husband's sister lives in Huelva and her husband is the Chief Librarian for the entire province. Through them, I got a phone number for Jésus Copeiro's wife and was able to contact her. She connected me to her husband and he sent me a copy of the William Martin book as well as answering my questions about William Watkins's involvement.

For his book, Copeiro interviewed Francis Haselden's daughters, who had a vivid memory of the handsome American aviator living in their house. They knew the story of the autopsy and Watkins's role in it, which consisted primarily of following Haselden's lead and saying as little as possible. Copeiro had also interviewed the fisherman who found Watkins and his plane upside down on the beach near Huelva. His dramatic account offered a strong sense of Watkins's personality.

William Anderson Watkins, was born on 9th May, 1920 in Corpus Christi, Texas to Ruth Harvin and John Tarleton Harvin. They had five sons: John, Tarleton (known as 'Jack'), Robert, William and Woodruff.

When William was two years old and Woodruff had not yet been born, their father died in Mexico leaving Ruth to raise five young boys. Four years later, Ruth Harvin married Colonel (then Major) Dudley Warren Watkins, an Army Air Corps officer and flight instructor who had taught Charles Lindbergh how to fly. Colonel Watkins adopted Ruth's boys and brought his son, Dudley Watkins, Jr, into the family. All six boys grew up on airfields in Texas, the Philippines and at Wright Patterson Field in Ohio, because of their father's military service.

Eventually, Colonel Watkins and all six of the Watkins sons would serve in the Armed Forces during World War Two. Four were aviators: John, Jack, William and Woody. Robert was an engineer who was killed when his ship was torpedoed on his way home from Iceland to go to Officers Training School. Dudley served as a tank officer in the China-Burma-India theatre of operations. Woody was killed in a flight training accident at Eagle Pass Army Air Field in Texas, just before receiving his wings in May 1944.

In the fall of 1939, William Watkins (*Operation Mincemeat*'s Willie, known to his family as Bill or Billy), enrolled at the University of Virginia in the College of Arts & Sciences. While we don't know much about his college career, the 1940 Virginia yearbook, *Corks and Curls*, does show him competing on the Freshman Swim Team and pledging the Sigma Chi fraternity. The following school year, his younger brother Woodruff joined him in Charlottesville. By this time, Bill was a full-fledged member of Sigma Chi and can be seen in the fraternity's group photo in the 1941 yearbook. The following school year (1941-1942), Woodruff is still listed at the University of Virginia, but William is not.

In the summer of 1941, William became eligible for World War Two draft registration indicated by the 'S' on his draft card. This was for 'males who had reached 21 since the first registration' on 16th October 1940. He had turned 21 on 9th May 1941. On his draft card, he crossed out 'EMPLOYER'S NAME AND ADDRESS' and wrote 'University of Virginia.' He listed his address in Arlington, Virginia, which was, and currently is, an upper-middle class neighbourhood of large homes in the Washington, D.C. suburbs – likely his parents' address. According to his brother John, Billy ultimately joined the RAF and went to England. He transferred to the U.S. Army Air Corps on Christmas, 1942.

Woody's draft card indicates that he was part of a draft for 'men born after 1st January 1922 and on or before 30th June 1924.' He gives his age as 19 which means that he had to have registered after his 19th birthday on 22nd October 1941. Yearbook listing notwithstanding, by that time, he had apparently left UVa for flight training at Embry Aero College in Florida as that is what he lists for "EMPLOYER."

The Watkins brothers participated in some of the most consequential fighting of World War Two. Jack was stationed at Hickam Field, Pearl Harbor, Hawaii in December 1941 and was one of the only pilots to get off the ground and chase the Japanese planes after the surprise attack. According to his brother, John, 'He wasn't shot up but the Japs (sic) certainly did a job of ruining his new convertible coupe.' From that statement it's possible to discern a bit of the attitude and swagger of the Watkins brothers.

Eventually, both John and Jack commanded P-40 squadrons in North Africa and crossed paths there. It was there, too, that John would eventually enter the Operation Mincemeat story.

But first, William Watkins had to crash land on the beach in Huelva.

The time that 'Willie' Watkins spent in Huelva encompasses only one paragraph in Ben Macintyre's book, quoted earlier, but the interviews conducted by the Spanish authors Jesús Copeiro and Enrique Nielsen shed light on how Watkins arrived in Huelva, spent his time while he was there, and how he eventually left.

On 27th April 1943, Watkins crash landed on the remote beach known as 'Barronal'. He had run out of fuel after hovering over the beach for half an hour, trying to find an appropriate place to land. His Airacobra fighter plane, '…suffered damage to the landing gear, leaving the propeller shattered, the left wing broken, the engine block broken, the fuselage with some broken plates and the tail rudder damaged.' Copeiro and Nielsen interviewed Antonio Macias, the fisherman who found his plane in the sand. Here is his account of Watkins's rescue:

I was a fisherman, we would go out to sea at night and sell in the afternoon.

Then I would go see my girlfriend at Portil, where she lived. We had to travel seven kilometres along the beach and as many back. My girlfriend was the daughter of Portuguese fishermen and she lived in the shacks on the beach. That day I saw a plane coming over the sea from El Portil and getting closer and lower, it turned around, observing the terrain, it landed on the beach, about four kilometres from Punta Umbría, in the area called 'Barronal', an area of dunes next to some pine forests. It was 4.30 in the afternoon. The plane plunged its nose into the sand, flipped over and ended up in an inverted position, leaving the pilot trapped in the cockpit. I ran towards him and through the glass window I could see the pilot's hand digging in the sand. The first thing I did was use the broken propeller to break the glass and let air in so he could breathe, then I tried to force the door to get him out, but I couldn't. I approached the dunes, took one of the wooden stakes, placed by the Forestry to hold the sand and protect the pine forests.

I inserted its edge into the slot in the pilot's sheet metal door and levered it up a bit, then I put my fingers and forcefully with my feet on the plane. I pulled hard and was able to open it. The pilot was face down, held by his seatbelt. Finally I used a dagger to cut the strap.

When he was free he embraced me. He was cut by glass and had a scratch on the cheek. The first thing he did was bathe in the sea. Nearby, a girl named Manuela was catching clams and when she observed the accident she ran out to notify the soldiers' barracks in Punta Umbría. The pilot's intention was to leave the place and go to Portugal, so with the help of a small silver coin that he applied to a slot, he opened a door and took out a suitcase. He changed his clothes and as we began the march the soldiers arrived, and we had to follow them along the beach.

Once in Punta Umbría my uncle José Suné Durán, a doctor, gave him the first medical treatment. The pilot spent a couple of days in the village. During the day he remained in the detachment, although he could go on horseback to the place where the plane crashed.

At night he slept in the Casino de la Esperanza. The wings of the plane were detached and the rest was dragged by the soldiers across the sand, using mules, employing stout sticks and hauling it to the Punta Umbría dock.

They removed the railing to the pier, placed the plane on a barge, taking advantage of high tide and took it to Huelva. There, with the help of the port cranes, it was put on a truck and taken to the Tablada air base. The pilot's name was Guillermo and he spent about a month staying at the British vice-consul's house in Huelva. He then left for Gibraltar, but before leaving he left an envelope with a photo inside and a written address for me to deliver. I wrote several times to North America, to the address, but never received a response. The vice consul confirmed his death in the war. For many years I kept the photo as a *souvenir, but the humidity ended up spoiling it and we threw it away.*

The Casino de la Esperanza, now a bar and restaurant, still exists on the beach in Huelva. At some point, Watkins was moved from the Casino to a hotel in Huelva called La Granadina. He was later moved to the home of Francis Haselden, the British Vice Consul in Huelva who took responsibility for his security. Haselden also plays a key role in the musical *Operation Mincemeat* as he is the only person in Spain who knows the truth about the corpse.

Watkins was invited to the autopsy of William Martin, which took place in a small building at Nuestra Señora de la Soledad cemetery on the outskirts of Huelva. Today, that cemetery is the site of William Martin's grave. By the time of the autopsy, the sea and the heat had done its worst as far as the corpse was concerned and Watkins was understandably eager to leave. It was quickly obvious to the Spanish authorities that there was no relationship between the two crashes and that Watkins knew nothing about Major William Martin. All that remained was for Haselden to complete the Operation Mincemeat mission by ensuring that the Spanish officers took possession of Martin's briefcase containing the misleading documents. MI5 believed that, if that happened, the documents would certainly end up in the hands of the Germans as Huelva was crawling with German spies.

According to Margaret Haselden, one of Francis Haselden's daughters, as quoted from an interview with Copeiro, there was some concern about whether Watkins might think he should safeguard the documents in Bill Martin's briefcase and prevent them from reaching Berlin. Apparently, he caught on to what Frances Haselden was doing and played along with the ruse, or at the very least, kept his mouth shut:

> My father had to be aware so as not to screw up the operation. When his friend, Mariano Pascual de Pobil, wanted to give him the briefcase with the documents, my father, who did not want to take it, had to react quickly and invent an excuse not to accept it and finally said to him: 'Well, perhaps, your superior will not like it, you should better give it to him first and then return it to me, thus following the official way.' In this way he gave time for it to be shown to the Germans first. A young American pilot was present with my father, whose plane had crashed in Huelva and since there was no American consulate in the city, he was staying at our house. The pilot was surprised by my father's attitude of not accepting the briefcase. Naturally he did not know anything about the matter, nor did my father clarify it to him, leaving my father as stupid in the eyes of the young pilot.

Stupid perhaps. But possibly Watkins had the sense that

there was something more going on and chose to play along with Haselden.

One could certainly imagine that it would have been pleasant for William Watkins to sit out the rest of the war with the Haseldens in Huelva. Photographs show him enjoying himself with the Haselden daughters and assorted British expats. But the Watkins family was always eager to serve and it was inevitable that he would return to duty as an Army Air Corps aviator. There is some difference of opinion as to how this came about. According to Copeiro and Neilsen, on 28th May 1943, Watkins was escorted by a Spanish aviation lieutenant, Rafael Losano Cotarelo, from Huelva to Gibraltar which was, of course, British territory. He was interned there but was picked up by his older brother, Captain John C.A. Watkins, who was Group Operations Officer for the 325th Fighter Group.

An article from the *Baltimore Evening Sun* dated 10th November 1943 tells a somewhat different story. In an interview with Captain John Watkins who was stateside to get married and had been the Aviation Editor of the *Sun* before the war, he said the following in reference to his brother: 'He crashed in Spain one day, was interned but escaped and wound up in Morocco. I heard he was there... so I flew to Morocco and found him and asked him to join our group.'

The story told by the Spanish authors and the fisherman seems, on the face of it, to be more believable for several reasons. One, it's difficult to envision how Watkins would have 'escaped' and 'returned to Morocco' in the midst of the war and in a very active theatre of operations. Two, one imagines that Margaret Haselden would have mentioned something as dramatic as an escape in her interview. Three, Gibraltar is just a short drive/flight/boat ride from Huelva and it would seem far easier for Francis Haselden to have arranged the transfer to a British-held enclave.

It is certain, however, that once reunited with his brother, William flew with his squadron in the Mediterranean theatre. As Captain John Watkins said in his *Sun* interview, 'He flew some missions with me. I didn't like the idea so much. It took my mind off the job. I was too busy counting the P-40s in Billy's flight.' Just over a month after Captain Watkins made this prescient statement, on Christmas Day 1943, William Anderson Watkins was flying in bad weather when he crashed into the side of a mountain in Foggia, Italy. He was 23 years old, meaning previous information about him claimed he was three years older than he would ever be.

The *Baltimore Sun*'s 17th February, 1944 obituary for William Anderson Watkins says the following, 'Early in 1943 he was forced down in Spain and interned. After several weeks, he managed to escape to North Africa and later joined the fighter group led by his brother John. The brothers flew together on numerous missions over Sicily and Italy.'

Because of John's professional relationship with *the Sun*, it's easy to surmise that his version of Watkins's 'escape' was used in the obituary. In 1944, after the deaths in action of his brothers William and Robert, John returned to the United States for good in accordance with the U.S. military's survivor policy:

In recognition of the Sacrifice and contribution made by a family which has lost two or more sons who were members of the armed forces, consideration will be given to the return to, or the retention in, the continental limits of the United States, of all remaining members of the immediate family.

William Watkins won the Air Medal with oak leaf clusters. At the time of his death, his brothers and father held, between them, two Distinguished Flying Crosses, three Air Medals with 20 oak leaf clusters and two Purple Hearts. It's interesting to note that, somehow, Francis Haselden must have followed Watkins's progress and was able to tell the fisherman, Antonio Macias, that 'Guillermo' had died in the war. In April 1949, his body was repatriated from Bari, Italy to the United States. Along with their father, Colonel Dudley Warren Watkins, he is interred in a family plot at Arlington National Cemetery.

There are four gravestones in Arlington. Three are grouped together: One is William Watkins's actual gravestone along with his brothers who also died in the war, Robert and Woodruff. The second is his brother Tarleton

(Jack) and third is his father Colonel Dudley Watkins. The other is the gravestone of John Watkins and his wife Izetta which includes the inscription, "Brothers Together Again - John-Jack- Bob-Bill-Woody."

CHAPTER TEN

THE BOX

THE relationships we had forged with the living members of the Leggatt family endured even after the plaque had been unveiled at the theatre. The following month, in January 2024, they reached out with some exciting news. Unknowingly, they had timed this particularly well. Another large Mincefluencer meet-up had been planned for 15th January, with numbers even higher than the first.

This second event had been dubbed 'Operation Human Thermos', in reference to a line in the show that sees Charles Cholmondeley describing the cannister designed to get Bill's body to Huelva as fresh as possible as 'the world's first human thermos'. Considering the expected cold temperatures of January, the title seemed fitting.

With so many people already assembling to attend the show as part of the meet-up, the researcher who had received the developments from the Leggatt family assembled a group of as many members of the

#FindingHester team as possible. We ended up in an office at Gray's Inn, gathered around a meeting room table, with no idea what we were about to be told. In the corner was a table of gin and tonics, an apt choice of refreshment considering the musical's Hester's reaction to hearing of the success of the mission is to proclaim 'I need a gin'.

It turned out, the Leggatts had more of Hester's things than they thought. Although there were no surviving pictures, it wasn't just the letter from the British Council that they had in their possession. While clearing out an office, a box had been uncovered.

It was rather a small box, made of cardboard and roughly the size of an A4 sheet of paper. The bottom was stamped 4 MAR 1958 and also, interestingly, but as far as we can tell, coincidentally, with a return address on St. James's Street – the same street Hester had worked on during the war at the MI5 London offices. The front of the box makes it clear it was Hester's. Addressed to 'Miss H Leggatt, 13 Beaufort Gdns, SW3', an address we already recognised, it was dated 11/1/43, three months before Operation Mincemeat was being planned and enacted.

The branding on the box belonged to Marshall & Snelgrove, a department store that had been around since 1837 and had merged with Debenhams in 1919, owing to financial trouble caused by World War One. They traded from the corner of Oxford Street and Vere Street and Hester had evidently shopped there. Now we were holding the box she had once held, but it was the contents that was more valuable to her, and now to us.

In the box, Hester had collected and kept a series of documents relating to World War Two. There were stacks of letters and two diaries. It was far more than we would have been able to look at in the short time we had before we all needed to get to the theatre for the show, so a plan was quickly devised.

First, G&Ts away. Now that there was archival material on the table, we weren't about to risk spilling drinks on it. Some concerns were raised about our lack of white cotton gloves to handle the documents, but the archivists in the room quickly shot down the myth. Porous gloves do nothing to protect handlers from potential mould on documents or documents from the oils on handlers' skin, and instead only impair the dexterity of your fingers and make you more likely to rip things. The safest thing to do was to touch these documents directly, just as Hester had touched them.

We quickly set up a system of photographing every single diary page and letter, dividing into small groups to efficiently process the documents in an assembly-line system. Reading and transcribing them all would come later. Despite rarely getting to meet in person, this was a group of people who had mastered the art of effective teamwork, and every single document was captured.

Also in attendance that evening was a journalist from *The Times*, seeking to do some research into the Mince-fluencers and their support of *Operation Mincemeat*. Our enthusiasm over the contents of an old box probably didn't help any arguments in favour of our sanity but he was kind enough to write a very nice article, so we can't have scared him too much.

Opening Hester's diaries was an incomprehensible experience. We had one from 1941 and one from 1943, the year of Operation Mincemeat. Eight months prior, the world had known next to nothing about this woman and we now had a record of every single day of her life for two years. They were more like appointment diaries than emotional ones, but they still revealed so much about her life.

In the back of the 1943 diary, Hester recorded a list of things she intended to do every night and at the very top was to spend five minutes working on her diary and appointments, and this resolution would work very much in our favour.

Reading older handwriting can take some getting used to, but we knew Hester's writing from 'Pam's' letters and from the documents we'd discovered through our research. The more we read of the diaries, the more the words became clear and we quickly transcribed an intimate window into Hester's life, significant not only to us because this was Hester and she mattered to us deeply, but also as a historical record of civilian life during World War Two.

The level of detail was astounding.

On the 5th of January 1943, she received one and a half pounds of sugar, two ounces of butter, half a pound of cheese, and margarine as her wartime rations. She also collected her laundry, annoyed to discover three hand-kerchiefs were missing, and lent a copy of *Fate Cannot Harm Me* to a friend called Enid. This was a novel by J.C. Masterman, who also makes an appearance in the *Operation Mincemeat* musical, also played by Jak Malone.

John Cecil Masterman was the chairman of the Twenty Committee, which oversaw the running of double agents in Britain during World War Two. Hester seems to have been reasonably well acquainted with Masterman, recording a little later, on 12th January, that it was 'J.C.'s birthday', which does indeed match up with the date he was born in 1891. It's one of very few birthdays that she records.

Days in work and days of leave are occasionally noted, especially in the 1941 diary which includes work schedules for Hester and four others, identified by the surnames Lefroy, Phillips, Elliott and Verel. Phillips seemed likely to be Margaret G Phillips, who Hester elsewhere refers to as Peggy. Hester attended her wedding to Christopher Harmer in the 1943 diary, on 6th March. Lefroy referred to Helen Lefroy, a woman who went on to become a Jane

Austen scholar and passed away in 2021, a few weeks after her 100th birthday. Verel was potentially Mary Verel, born 1921, but no further information on her could be found, and Elliott proved too common a surname to narrow down a candidate.

Considering the deaths of Hester's close family occurring so close together and leaving her without them all when she was fairly young, we couldn't help but start to worry about her, but we shouldn't have bothered. Hester's social life was incredibly busy, with the name of a new friend on almost every page as she planned activities with them: 'Lunch & French picture exhibition with Joan', 'Coffee with Alex', 'Lunch with Jill', 'Drink with George at Denmark & met Gemma', 'Tea with Helen', 'Lunch with Prue', 'Supper with Hazel', 'Dinner with Penelope', 'Coffee with Katherine', 'Dine with Allison', 'Heather's party', 'Lunch with Joselyn and Griselda', 'Lunch with Geoffrey'.

We couldn't track down the identities of most of these people, considering Hester only provided their first names, but she was clearly close enough to them to refer to them informally and schedule casual meetings with them. It seemed likely that Geoffrey might be Geoffrey Greig, whose wedding she attended in 1928, given that Esme, his wife, also makes several appearances in the documents.

Jak Malone once professed to specifically having created his Hester to have a social life that the show barely scratched the surface of, with a whole host of out of work activities to keep her busy. He couldn't have known at the time just how right he was.

One of the pastimes Hester frequently partook in throughout 1941 and 1943 was the playing of bridge. Played by two competing pairs, this card game is still one of the most popular in the world, however it is a lot more common amongst older generations as its height of popularity was in the 1940s, so it really should have been no surprise to us to find Hester playing it. Nevertheless, it delighted us, as it was another one of those little coincidences that also occurs in the musical.

SpitLip's Hester is a keen player of bridge, describing it to Jean as a 'wonderful game, endless variety, countless permutations', before going on to use it to teach the lesson that 'success always boils down to one thing: learning to play the hand that you're dealt. No matter how much one might want to win, you have to accept that others may always hold the trump cards.' Finding the same game mentioned repeatedly in Hester's diaries was a moment of serendipity. It felt like Hester might appreciate its inclusion in the show.

Hester was living with her mother during the war and the 'M' that she frequently went out to dinner with is almost certainly Jessie Leggatt, with the 'M' standing for 'mother'. They went to the cinema together and on several short holidays around England, suggesting a close relationship between mother and daughter. In one instance, on 9th July 1941, Hester recorded that she 'Lunched with M[other], Donald and Connie at Trocadero. Donald behaving like a baby because I wouldn't tell him where I worked. Result: he wouldn't talk to me at all. He leaves for the East tonight.'

'Donald' referred to her eldest brother, and 'Connie' to Constance Hadfield Olive, his second wife. That Hester went out for dinner with the pair and referred to Constance rather informally suggests she approved of, or at the very least tolerated, their relationship. Hester's adherence to the rules which governed her work and how much she could talk about it is commendable, but in this case it might have cost her something significant she would only come to realise over a year later. This could well have been the last time Hester ever saw her brother, before he left for Egypt, and passed away in 1942. Had she known, they might both have spent the time in a way other than bickering and sulking.

The Trocadero was far from the only restaurant Hester visited. Rationing was introduced to Britain in January 1940, controlling how much you could buy of different foods in order to maintain a fair and sustainable distribution. Hester often recorded her rations in her diaries and noted frequent periods when she was unable to get milk. Eating in restaurants, however, was 'off ration' so, for those who had the money, it meant access to meals that were often better than what could be made at home. Understandably, this was unpopular with those who could not afford meals out.

To prevent these restaurants raising prices to exploit the situation and cater only to the richest customers, the government introduced a maximum price tag of five shillings for a restaurant meal. Despite this, establishments would often try to circumvent this flat charge for food by putting on a number of additional charges for things like live music, dancing, or entrance fees to the building.

Regardless of what restaurants were charging for their meals, however, some things just couldn't be bought for any sum as food shortages got worse. Meat was often the first thing to disappear from a menu of an evening, with diners purposefully going early to try to claim their portion of what little the restaurant had been able to source.

It's understandable, then, that Hester was dining out so often. Some of the places she visited still exist today, including The Good Intent pub in Hornchurch, Essex. It is now run by Greene King, but in World War Two it was considered a favoured establishment for those stationed at the nearby RAF Hornchurch. Similarly, The Spread Eagle pub in Etwall, Derby is still trading.

Not everywhere still exists, however. Hester frequently visits La Sperenza, which might suggest it was near where she lived or worked, but it doesn't seem to have survived 80 years. Café Noel is another name that is no longer familiar. 'L'Aperitif' is likely L'Aperitif Grill, which was photographed in 1947 but cannot be found in modern day London.

The National Gallery canteen is a more recognisable name, referring to a predecessor to the restaurant found there today. During World War Two, the National Gallery was closed, along with many other galleries, museums, music halls and theatres, in order to avoid mass casualties of visitors during a bombing raid. The paintings were evacuated out of London and into storage, leaving the space empty. Pianist Myra Hess began a series of concerts in the Gallery, turning it into a concert venue for the duration of the war, and into 1946, with performances every weekday by Hess and fellow performers. These concerts were hugely popular in a capital desperate for cultural pursuits.

Observing these lunchtime concerts, Lady Irene Gater recognised the need for some catering and had set up a sandwich bar in the Tuscan Room by 1939. This venture was so popular that Gater launched an additional space in the basement, a canteen serving hot meals to civil servants and military personnel. It was here that Hester, a civil servant owing to her job at MI5, visited, recording the meal in her diary.

Hester also finds herself at The Ivy, a restaurant you can still visit today, although ownership has changed hands multiple times since. Originally founded in 1917, its location opposite the Ambassadors Theatre and St Martin's Theatre made it a popular destination for theatre actors and workers. It was an establishment Hester held in high regard, deeming it 'Excellent'.

A visit to 'Cordon Bleu' could well have been a trip to Au Petit Cordon Bleu at 11 Sloane Street, a restaurant attached to Le Cordon Bleu culinary school. The school was closed during the war, but the restaurant remained operational, creating dishes from substituted ingredients owing to the constraints of food shortages.

With how specific Hester often is about the places she visits, you could put together a food tour of London, and beyond, that calls at all her favoured restaurants that still survive.

It wasn't just dining out that filled Hester's leisure time. She recorded visits to the cinema, including a trip to see the film *Now, Voyager*, starring Bette Davis and Paul Henreid. The box also contained her review of Laurence Olivier's *Henry V*:

> *I enjoyed [it] very much, though it didn't quite come up to my expectations. It was in colour, much better colour than usual, but Laurence Olivier, although he looks the part & at moments is very good in it, is not quite equal to the long speeches, which I thought sounded a little uninspiring.*

She also seemed fond of the theatre, attending the

first night of Ivan Turgenev's *A Month in the Country*, at St. James's Theatre, which then stood on King Street. In 1944, she attended the West End revival of Noel Coward's *Private Lives* at the Apollo Theatre, deeming it 'most amusing & not a bit dated'. Not just attending plays, she also went to see *Sweet And Low*, a musical review of sketches, dances and songs at the Ambassadors Theatre. Perhaps she would have enjoyed *Operation Mincemeat*, if she had ever gotten to see it.

From the comfort of her own home she listened to *The Brains Trust*, a BBC radio programme featuring a panel of experts answering audience-provided questions. Clearly not wanting to miss an episode, she marked off which day to stay in for.

Hester also used her diary to record her daily chores and to do lists. She wrote of a lace blouse that was being made or altered by a 'Mrs Vine', as she recorded fitting appointments. Mending, ironing, washing underwear and shaving are all recorded. An extended attempt to procure a specific foundation cream from Harrods spans multiple entries. 4th March 1943 provided an entire list of things she had to accomplish before a trip to Fleet the next day:

> *Ev[enin]g. at home* ✓
> *Wash brushes* ✓
> *Pay Miss T.* ✓
> *Mend hair b[rush] cover* ✓

Lace blouse
White nightie?
Spotted nightie ✓
Black sandal ✓
Buttons on ✓
Tweed coat ✓
Clean brown gloves (polish)
Pack for Fleet

Entries like this allow us to get a sense of exactly what the day-to-day life of Hester May Murray Leggatt looked like, when previously no one had even known her true name. She recorded daily minutiae that not only gives a sense of daily life for the average person during World War Two, which is in itself a valuable record, but to us specifically, about this woman, this was priceless.

Even a list informing us that she spent nine pence on ribbon, 10 pence on sandwiches for dinner and two shillings on fudge told us so much. It allowed us to know Hester in a way we never expected. Nine months prior to this, none of us would have envisaged being able to conclusively say that Hester had a sweet tooth, but she frequently mentioned buying sweets when she could get them in wartime London.

When we initially combed through the diaries, we noticed multiple entries referring to Kate. Considering Hester's busy social calendar, we assumed this was another close friend that perhaps lived out of London, as many of the entries suggested she was coming to visit: 'Kate arrived', or 'Kate due'. However, looking more closely at some of the wording and the frequency of the mentions, it became clear from entries such as 'Kate started last night' that this was the term Hester used to refer to her period in her diary, so she could keep track of her cycle. It seemed there was no part of Hester's life that we didn't now have a window into.

While we were incredibly fond of the mundane elements of Hester's life we found recorded in her diaries, there were a few entries that stood out specifically for their departure from the mundane, often raising more questions than they answered.

On Tuesday 8th February 1943, Hester not only attended the wedding of her work friend Peggy, but also had arranged to go to the Old Bailey, the Central Criminal Court, to give evidence regarding the theft of her fur and lighter. This seems to have originally been tentatively scheduled for the Friday before, but Hester crossed this out. She noted that the Old Bailey postponed *sine die* in the entry for the 8th, and if it was rearranged in 1943, she didn't make note of it. The Old Bailey Proceedings were published from 1674 until April 1913, but they were no longer being produced by 1943, so any further details of the theft Hester was victim of have not come to light.

The 7th July 1941 also features a particularly detailed

entry, one of those that moves from appointment diary to a daily record of events and thoughts. Hester records 'Angela Robertson in to coffee and cool drinks after dinner. She taught me some dancing steps. I enjoyed having her.'

The identity of Angela Robertson is unclear, but the image of her being taught to dance inevitably reminded us of the choreography of Jean's song *All the Ladies* in the musical, in which Hester is dragged into a dance with the other MI5 secretaries against her will. Perhaps she would have been more adept than SpitLip imagined.

Another entry that gave us pause appears at first to be a list of strange, unrelated statements that are at odds with almost everything else in the diaries:

'Invitation to dine or theatre in a few days – by letter. Dark man (repeatedly), death satisfactory to me. Some money. I get my wish but not my second wish. Business letter wh[ich] will make me furious, but [dark] haired man helps to solve.'

We considered perhaps that this could be a recorded dream, as it seemed too out of place to be a record of genuine events, but on closer inspection it appears to be a record of Hester having her fortune told, with these concepts the predictions for her future. On at least one other occasion Hester notes 'Fortune told by Clare', so it seems like this might have been something she dabbled in on occasion, although she does elsewhere profess a disbelief for the spiritual.

In another document in the box, Hester writes 'I had my hand read by a Dutchman, quite amusingly & somewhat embarrassingly, but mostly nonsense, of course', with the words '& somewhat embarrassingly' being added above the line as an afterthought, perhaps in an attempt to distance herself from the act and any possible belief in it. Supernatural beliefs were not uncommon in Britain at this time. Spiritualism had been embraced after World War One as a way to deal with the grief and loss felt by the nation after the deaths of so many. A lot of people visited mediums in an attempt to connect with deceased loved ones.

Even the Special Operations Executive was not immune, hiring an astrologer who persuaded the likes of Admiral John Godfrey, Director of Naval Intelligence, that he could use horoscopes to both predict and influence Hitler's actions. Louis De Wohl, the astrologer in question, was sent on a lecture tour in America to convince the public that Hitler would be defeated, using horoscopes as his evidence.

Fortune-tellers were popular as, feeling powerless in the face of another war, people went looking for information about the futures of their loved ones off fighting. They wanted guarantees of safe return, of course, and fortune-tellers who predicted otherwise were seen to be a detriment to public morale and were often arrested. Whether Hester trusted the outcomes or not, she does seem to have been interested in the process of both palm-reading and fortune-telling, even if she pretended not to be.

One last thing in Hester's diary that caught our eye was the entry from 9th July 1941, where she records that she 'bathed in the light of the full moon. Deliciously cool & refreshing & mysterious. Drove back in front with George & he kissed me goodnight very tender & sweet'. Nothing could really seem further away from the elderly Hester Leggett of the 2021 *Operation Mincemeat* film than a night-time swim in a river and a goodnight kiss.

Jean might have thought her a draconic spinster, but Hester's life beyond the MI5 office was rich and vibrant with culture, friends, and love, and we were only just scratching the surface of what the box could tell us.

CHAPTER ELEVEN

DEAR VAL

HESTER'S role in the Operation Mincemeat story was that of the author of two fictitious love letters, intended to help sell the ruse of William Martin, giving MI5's made up man a backstory. So, when we realised it was love letters that made up the majority of the contents of the box in front of us on the table at Gray's Inn, it was almost unbelievable.

Even after we had begun our research on Hester, contemporary articles reporting on our work were still describing her as a woman who had never known love herself, all because she died unmarried. Now Hester herself had left us irrefutable evidence that she had been the perfect person at MI5 to write love letters to a soldier, because she'd written hundreds of them herself, and this recipient had been real.

Valdemar Bertie Caroe, known to Hester as Val, was born on 25th January 1892 in Riga, then part of Russia, but now the capital city of Latvia. His father, Anoton Axel Ferdinand Caroe was Danish, while his mother, Mary Caroe, was originally British. Val was therefore born a Danish citizen but was naturalised as a British citizen in 1914, at which time he was living at 21 Sandyford Place, Glasgow. 22 years old at the outbreak of World War One, Val joined the 3rd battalion of the Connaught Rangers, receiving both wounds and medals as a result of fighting in France.

In 1926, Val married a Maltese woman named Inez Rose Parnis, who herself had previously married a William O'Brien in 1908, with whom she'd had multiple children. You'll be relieved to know this is the final William of the story. Electoral rolls for Kensington and Chelsea record Val and Inez living together at 132 Oakwood Court in 1935, 1936 and 1937, with the 1939 Register confirming that they were still living together in September 1939.

Hester considered 25th November 1939 to be the start of her relationship with Val, noting down on that date in her 1941 diary that it was their second anniversary. Val never divorced his wife, but he would go on to have a relationship with Hester that lasted at least until 1945.

It isn't clear exactly where the pair met, although they did both live in Kensington at the time. Hester wasn't yet employed by MI5, but exactly where she was working is unclear. If her 'private secretary' occupation in the 1939 Register refers to her work for Sitwell, then it is very possible she was still working for him two months later when she met Val. We spent a lot of our research trying to work out exactly how Hester may have come to work for MI5, but many of the theories relied on several degrees of separation between Hester and someone high up in the Secret Service. Val might just be the answer. Her relationship with him started seven months before her employment, so it is possible that in spending time with him, Hester met the right people. She was extremely qualified to work in the War Office, with St James's Secretarial College being a highly-regarded organisation that supplied many MI5 secretaries, and with six years of experience as secretary to Sitwell, so the combination of being in the right place at the right time and having a very respectable CV might have opened the door to MI5 for her.

In March 1941, Val was posted to Northern Ireland in the role of army liaison to MI5, but he was promoted to Major and moved back to England to work for Section B1D, conducting interrogations of defectors and spies, including Columbine and Harlequin, code names for Hans Zech-Nenntwich, an SS officer, and Richard Wurmann, a German intelligence officer.

Val shows up frequently in Hester's diaries at this time, noted as often accompanying Hester to dinner. On their second anniversary, they attend the George Black musical *Get a Load of This* at the London Hippodrome on Charing Cross Road, now a casino. She also specified the nights he was fire watching, often doing so in a way that suggested she was annoyed at the inconvenience of not being able to spend time with him. Fire watching had been voluntary at the start of the war, with people often positioned on the rooftops of buildings in urban areas to keep watch for fires started by incendiary bombs, and to assist with putting them out. In September 1940, however, the government issued a Fire Watchers Order, under which men could be compelled to assist with fire watching for up to 48 hours a month. It's unclear whether Val was volunteering or had been co-opted under this Order.

A great deal about the ins and outs of Hester and Val's relationship can be gathered from the pages of Hester's diaries, but it is the letters in the box that most accurately paint the picture of their time together. Val's letters were all carefully kept in their original envelopes, just as Hester would have received them, but there were also a number of letters from Hester herself. These exist as draft copies of letters that she sent to Val, with her often practising the same letter more than once, in order to best arrange the content before writing a final version. Some pages contain checklists of topics she was seeking to cover, with many featuring sentences or paragraphs that she crossed out as part of the drafting process. One even features some charming doodles, with Hester absentmindedly drawing circles and grids over her words.

The letters that are dated are from 1944 and 1945,

although not all of them come with years attached, and many are sent between England and France, with Val stationed in Paris and Hester still working in London. Comparing Hester's letters to 'Pam's' letters from Major William Martin's briefcase makes it undoubtedly clear who penned them. The words are, of course, different, but the hand is unquestionably the same.

Together with the diaries, Hester's letters tell us even more about who she was as a person. Both the 1941 and 1943 diaries feature Hester lending out books to friends and ordering new publications, but one letter demonstrates even more clearly her love for reading:

I have at last managed to finish G.M. Young's 'English Social History' – over six hundred pages – and then I read 'Three Men in a Boat', just for fun, because it was about the river and brings in so many of the places we know. Now I am reading a book about Jane Austen and a new and rather good novel, both at once.

By 'G.M. Young' she likely means 'G.M. Trevelyan', who had written the history of six hundred centuries of England up until 1900. *Three Men in a Boat (To Say Nothing of the Dog)* is an 1889 comedic novel by Jerome K Jerome, concerning a boating holiday on the Thames. In the four books Hester describes, she covers a range of topics and genres. Presumably she was not at this point imagining there would one day be a book about her.

With the letters allowing us to work out who exactly this 'Val' was who appeared in the diaries, we were able to read some of the entries with a newly-acquired context, like this one from 14th July 1941:

> *Val was late, though only just after me, & he went & had dinner at La Sperenza, went home to work & found he had left his glasses chez moi. He rang me up & there they were. He insisted on coming for them, it was nearly 10, he stayed to hear Churchill's speech (very good) & I made us coffee. He left about 10.45, after we had tried & failed to get a taxi because of the rain. Rather fun!*

The speech Hester mentions is Churchill's *Do Your Worst and We'll Do Our Best* speech, given at a luncheon for the London County Council at County Hall. In it, Churchill speaks directly to Hitler, proclaiming: 'We will have no truce or parley with you, or the grisly gang who work your wicked will. You do your worst and we will do our best.' With the Blitz only considered over since May 1941, he also professed the resilience of Britain's capital: 'If the lull is to end, if the storm is to renew itself, London will be ready, London will not flinch, London can take it again.' Hester, who had lived in the city throughout the Blitz, likely believed deeply in its strength and courage.

So much is often made of people remembering where they were at exact moments, so to know Hester was home with someone she loved as she was reminded that London may once again face an onslaught of bombs is a window into both her relationship, and the life she was living in wartime Britain.

The knowledge of exactly who Val was also informed how we read Hester's diary entry for 10th July 1941: 'Val round to me for a drink. Told him about Kate (7th).' Given that we know 'Kate' is how Hester referred to her period, this specific record of her telling Val that 'Kate' had arrived on the 7th seems like it may have been the relieved end to a pregnancy scare. Despite Hester's lengthy relationship with Val, they were unmarried and he still legally had a wife. Falling pregnant would have put Hester in a difficult situation.

Even with Val already married, it seems that his relationship with Hester was an open secret, if it was even a secret at all. The 1943 diary features Hester and Val going to Wargrave, where they met Guy Liddell, Head of Section B at MI5, and Hugh Astor, who was employed in Section B1A. There is never any suggestion in Hester's writings that they would have to hide in public, or that running into her boss was anything to be concerned about.

On one occasion, Hester relays a story to Val over letter that only reaffirms the notion that they seem to have been open about the fact they were a couple. She was staying in Hove with her mother and, on going out to tea, ran in to two people that she knew she recognised but could not remember the names of. After a rather relatable tale of awkwardly avoiding having to introduce them to her mother, Hester says: 'of course they asked after you & as they said goodbye she turned back & asked to be remembered to you', something she couldn't do as she didn't really remember the woman herself. It made for an amusing anecdote to share in a letter, but it also makes it clear that this woman, whoever she was, knew how closely Val and Hester were acquainted. Given that Hester couldn't remember her name, the relationship was obviously not confined to the knowledge of only close friends.

Many of the stories Hester shared in her letters concerned people with whom they were both mutually acquainted with at MI5. Just as SpitLip's Hester explains in her lecture to Jean and Cholmondeley on the writing of love letters, 'when you're writing to someone you love, far away, you want […] them to feel as normal as possible, as though they're going to come home and it's all going to go back to how it was before.' To achieve that, 'you start with news.' And the real Hester did:

> *Max K has recently married a girl called Susie Barnes who was at Oxford, in the Registry, I think, & there is some difference of opinion as to who has made a Big mistake. So there you have a nice cross-section of office gossip to take your mind off your troubles.*

This was Hester trying to make Val feel as normal as

possible while he was abroad and complaining about struggling with the language or being bitterly cold and lacking enough warm clothes.

Some other mentions of the office are, however, less concerned with gossip about coworkers and more of a whine about how much time they had to spend apart:

> It does seem very unfair to have prevented you from getting another job & taken you away from London, & then when you were out of reach in France to let it all drift. I do think that is rather a black mark against our office – the right job so seldom seems to be found for the right man – or woman.

It's unclear whether the addition of 'or woman' at the end is simply Hester acknowledging the many women who also worked at MI5, or whether she felt that she too had not been placed in the right job. There is little else in the documents to suggest any real lack of job satisfaction, but all of her letters to Val would have been read by censors, so complaining about her position at MI5 in them would probably have been unwise.

It's possible that, just like SpitLip's Jean, Hester felt frustrated to be consigned to the role of secretary in an office where all the positions that came with any real power were held by men, but the letters never provide any further insight into the matter.

Hester might not have been specifically complaining

about her role at MI5, but she did discuss the complaints that other MI5 employees had with each other:

I've been working rather hard this week as TAR's secretary is on leave, but as it hardly ever stops raining for a minute I haven't missed much by being in the office. You say I never mention J.C. – it's chiefly because he's not worth mentioning at the moment – very moody & difficult. I really think he is ill – he seems to get thinner & older looking every day, poor old thing. Also I'm afraid he resents my working for Hugh Astor & feels he isn't getting enough attention. Unfortunately all our officers sit together now in the same dark & overcrowded room. Poor Hugh suffers tortures as he has a mania for fresh air, & J.C. & Marriott guard the windows like dragons & will never allow them to be opened when they are there! So poor Hugh sits there getting greyer and greyer in the face & coming up for air every now & then. He's rather a dear.

This extract contains a whole host of familiar names: J.C. is once again John Masterman, chairman of the Twenty Committee, and TAR refers to Thomas Argyll Robertson, a Scottish MI5 intelligence office who was known frequently by his initials, and who was responsible for Double Cross.

TAR also makes a small appearance in *Operation Mincemeat*, played by Claire-Marie Hall at the start of the show and up until *God That's Brilliant*, in which various MI5 employees plot how best to kill Hitler. Claire's character did, however, have to acquire the fictitious first name 'Reggie', as some audience members unfamiliar with the names on the payroll at MI5 were mistaking 'TAR' for the word 'ta', the shortened form of 'thank you', so he lives on as Reginald Tar.

The perspective this letter gives into the MI5 offices is a very human one. Here were men dealing with some of the most secret information of the war, and they were squabbling over windows. As much as it rather punctures the almost mythical status of the wartime work of the Secret Service, it's a delightful look into Hester's daily life at work. One of the other characters who shows up is John Marriott, who would later become director of MI5's B branch and presumably was then pleased to be in the position to give more orders than he took, considering his dissatisfaction with a work trip to Brussels:

Marriott is going to Brussels, fairly soon I think – he doesn't know yet for how long, but he looks nearly as pleased at the prospect as the man is in the condemned cell – a really pathetic sight! He will be shaken out of his cosy little B1A groove, which will be bad enough, of course, & then, as he openly says, 'I hate the Continent!'

Hester and Val's relationship might have been fairly illicit, considering it was happening out of wedlock and involved an already married man, but it carries all the hallmarks of a domestic relationship between a married couple. Hints of jealousy shine through as Hester instructed Val to 'take care of yourself, and don't let your collection of beautiful and lovely Ats, Wrafs and princesses cause too many flutters in your susceptible heart', referring to the Women's Royal Air Force and Auxiliary Territorial Service women that Val would have been working with. Presumably she didn't mention the kiss she received from George that she mentioned in her diary on 9th July 1941, over a year and a half into her relationship with Val.

Most of her letters were more concerned with Val's wellbeing than jealousy, however, and particularly with whether he was keeping warm enough. In one letter she wrote:

I do hope you have enough warm things with you. Let me know if I can get anything for you, or if you would like me to knit you another sweater. But remember you must send me your sizes for anything you want. I saw a very fetching little leather waistcoat lined with lamb's wool in a shop in St. James's Street the other day. The only trouble about that would be that your lower half would probably feel comparatively colder!

It seems at this point that Val's relationship with his wife was functionally over, if Hester was the one offering to shop for him in England and knit him warm jumpers. By the writing of this letter, it seems she had already knitted him at least one. She was also the one offering to send him newspapers so he has something to read:

I have just sent off today's Telegraph to you, & wonder whether you would like me to send it every day, & the S[unday] Times every week? I have just had your letter written on the 18th in which you say you hardly ever see a paper, & that gave me the idea, thought I can't imagine why I didn't think of it before!

Although she promises in later letters that sending the newspaper every day would be no trouble at all, she would still have to have gone to the time and expense of tracking one down every day, addressing it, and dropping it in the post box, but this effort is negated in the face of her concern that Val should have access to the daily newspaper. She also sent over a tobacco pouch, to store loose tobacco for rolling, in the draft of a letter dated 16th March:

Here at last is your tobacco pouch, darling – I am so sorry you haven't had it sooner, I didn't know that your present one was in such a desperate state, & I hoped to see you again very soon to give it to you. It comes with my best love though very late, I am afraid, for your birthday.

Messages on birthdays and Christmases are a common theme to the letters, just as they would be between any separated husband and wife, with Hester beginning one of the few of her draft letters that bears a date with 'This is to wish you very many happy returns on your birthday,

Hester's mother and brother Bill are the two closest living relatives she had by the time these letters were being written, and they frequently pop up, often together, in tales of home, suggesting that Val had met them both, or at least heard enough about them to feel like he had. While contemplating the delayed arrival of Val's luggage in France, Hester shared that *'Bill never got his heavy luggage back again — it simply vanished, though his of course was a very different and much longer journey,'* likely referring to his journey to North Africa in 1942.

She also wrote to Val to inform him of the events of the day her brother collected his Distinguished Service Order:

Great excitement to-day, brother Bill has gone with Connel and Mother to Buckingham Palace to collect his D.S.O. Poor Mama was in rather [a] flutter, because although she was longing to go, it meant leaving the house at 9 a.m., and as she doesn't usually get down to breakfast until about a quarter to ten, it was going to be something of an effort! She had also heard from a friend of hers whose son was decorated recently that she had to queue up with hundreds of other[s] for half an hour in the rain beforehand! Luckily it wasn't raining this morning, so I hope she enjoyed it.

The word 'Connel' had originally been written as 'his wife', but the correction to her name suggests that Val knew enough about Bill to recognise his wife's name.

Hester's dedication to keeping Val up to date with the lives of her family suggests she wanted him to be a part of it. She shared not only major events, such as the collecting of the D.S.O., but also more minor updates: *'Mother has heard from Bill that he has been having fibrositis + flu both at the same time, poor thing, + suffering agonies.'*

Illness in general is another fairly common theme of the letters, with Hester both recounting her own illnesses and enquiring after Val's recovery from his own: *'How is your cold, darling my dear − have you really got rid of it? I do wish I could look after you.'*

One particular letter, written during a snowy winter, features a desire to stay in bed that many would be able to find relatable:

> *I'm writing this in bed as I have suddenly started a bad cold, & unless I stay away from the office for a day or so now it may drag on for weeks. There's really no need for me to be actually in bed, but it's rather warm & comfy, especially as there was snow last night & this morning − it is now lying one inch thick outside.*

With people's diets impacted by rationing and disruptions to food import channels, illness like colds were more common than usual. Many people also struggled to find adequate fuel to heat their homes, so it is no surprise that Hester wrote of waves of illness plaguing her entire office at MI5:

There was a sudden epidemic of [colds] at the office last week & when I got back after two days away & found everyone spluttering & croaking all around me I nearly turned tail & went back to bed again.

It appears that Hester was possibly particularly suscep-tible to bouts of illness, some of which were minor colds and some of which manifested with more serious flu-like symptoms. The worst illness she describes in her draft letters to Val had her out of work for a full week:

You must forgive the squiggly writing, as I am sitting up in bed drawing on my knees. Yes – once more! On Monday at the office I suddenly had a violent attack of shivering which I couldn't stop. My teeth chattered & I felt wretched. Dr Page very kindly drove me back in his car & by the time I got home my temp was 102 & I could hardly summon up enough energy to undress, fill a hot water bottle, & get into bed. I had a very bad night but the doctor came next day & though my temp was 102 again in the middle of the day it went down a little in the evening & is under 100 today. However I'm not allowed to go back to work til next week, so I foresee five more days of boredom.

Jak Malone once asked us if we had ever found anything to say that Hester was particularly thin, as it was something a visiting Leggatt descendent at stage door had once mentioned to him, and Hester was able to answer the question herself in one of her letters to Val in which she recalls a meeting with a doctor:

The doctor was very cross with me because he said I was much too thin, & I very nearly told him that I would be both fitter and fatter after a spell of leave with you.

This seems to be a frequent complaint that Hester's doctor had with her, and at one point he provided her with the prescription of extra rations of milk in an attempt to increase her weight:

I am up again now, I'm thankful to say & go back to work tomorrow. Luckily it was a short & sharp attack instead of the slow lingering kind which some people seem to be getting. The doctor has given me a certificate for extra milk & I am now supposed to drink a quart a day for the next three months! That alone ought to put on an inch or two round my waist!

Despite Val's frequent and lengthy absences from London, Hester was not left alone to suffer through her illnesses. Her wide network of friends and her mother, although often also ailing, would provide any assistance she needed, including donations of valuable rationed produce:

Mother, who was only allowed out of her room for the first time yesterday, insisted on coming round to see me, which was very naughty of her, & everyone is being very kind, giving me eggs & oranges & offering to do things for me. How I hate being in bed on these glorious sunny days!

In the *Operation Mincemeat* musical, Hester walks in on Jean and Cholmondeley attempting to write the 'Pam' letters together and failing miserably, with it being implied that neither of them have ever been in love, so they both have no idea how to write love letters. After witnessing their overly effusive and saccharine exclamations that 'love is a bird, building a nest in my heart', Hester questions them with 'is that really how you think people write to each other?' She has opinions about how love letters are to be written. As, evidently, did the real Hester, because she writes Val a fairly specific breakdown of how she thinks his letters could be improved:

I don't think that I need explain to you the kind of letters I like to get from you – you used to know how to write them all right. You know, quite well, that I never find your letters dull – only rather unsatisfying sometimes.
[…]

In case you really don't understand what I mean I will just say that I hope the length of your letters + the number of times you write to me don't depend on the number of parties you go to. I like to hear what you are doing, but I also like to hear what you are thinking + feeling + hoping for as well.
[…]

> *It would be rather nice to know if you are missing me*
> *+ looking forward to seeing me + what you are planning*
> *for us. Do I really have to tell you all this?*

It is true that Hester's letters are often a lot more personal than the ones she receives in return, although we do of course only have her working copies to go on. Exactly what she sent to Val is unknown, but considering these thoughts on the things a letter to a lover ought to contain, it seems like the real Hester's letters would have matched the standards of the SpitLip's Hester.

An affinity for writing love letters is perhaps something that could have been guessed about Hester from the start, considering her writing of the 'Pam' letters is one of the few things that was known about her, but based on the contents of the letters the writing team behind the musical got a few other things correct as well. One of the motifs Hester has in the show is a rose and, while there's nothing quite that specific, an appreciation of flowers does come through, with mentions of crocuses, violets and primroses blooming in the spring.

The musical's Hester also approves, with some prompting from Jean, of being memorialised in 'a grand royal park', so it was particularly enjoyable to read of the real Hester visiting St James's Park, close to her office:

> *We have had such lovely sunny spring days lately that it*
> *has been an agony going out of it all into the stuffy office*

to work. Today has been simply perfect – not a cloud in the sky all day & quite warm enough to sit outside! The willows round the lake in St. James's Park are first out & look as though they had been powdered with pale green!

Just like there was in the diaries, there are also pleasingly coincidental mentions of bridge, with a reference to Val playing in France:

You seem to be having plenty of bridge – what a good thing you don't always lose nowadays! How you can concentrate on the cards & organise your French at the same time is beyond me.

Considering how little they had to work with, SpitLip were right on the money with some of their characterisations.

It wasn't all charming walks in St James's Park and blooming flowers, however. Hester and Val were still living through a war and their various frustrations with how the conflict impacted their lives appear in much of their correspondence. Many of their letters criticise the time it took post to be delivered, with multiple letters often turning up all at once despite being dated as sent days apart. As Hester complains:

I don't at all approve of the long gaps in between & then when I get so many in a bunch I can't answer them properly. However I suppose it's just one of those things that one grumbles at but can't do anything much about.

She also specifically mentions that one of Val's letters had been censored, although this was not a common problem for them. Almost all of the envelopes containing the letters sent to Hester are stamped either with a purple or red shield containing the words 'PASSED BY CENSOR' and then an identification number of which employee read and approved the letter; or with a blue circular stamp reading 'RELEASED BY BASE CENSOR' and the date. Hester and Val were both aware of what they could and couldn't say, but that didn't mean they enjoyed the restrictions, or that they believed they all made sense. At one point Hester questioned the limitations on Val's ability to tell her about his work:

Are you sure it is still so hush about where you go & so on? After all, the Germans must know it when they see you there, so who is it we're trying to deceive? And some people seem to be able to say much more in letters from the Continent & other places abroad. But you know best about what you can say of course.

Although the days of the Blitz were over by 1944 and 1945, when it seems most of the letters were written, London would still experience further bombing. In June 1944, V-1s were launched at London. These flying bombs came with plyboard wings and an engine to propel them across the Channel from sites in occupied France. They were nicknamed doodlebugs, owing to the buzzing sound the engines made as they propelled the bombs overhead. It was when the sound stopped that people needed to worry, with the bombs then falling quickly towards the ground.

In September, London also suffered the effects of bombing from V-2 rockets. These were revenge attacks, designed to destroy vast parts of London and the morale of its citizens. These were ballistic missiles, more expensive and slower to make, but more deadly. Although they often inspired less fear in those targeted, as they lacked the ominous buzz of the doodlebugs.

The continuation of attacks with both V-1 and V-2 bombs meant air raid sirens still pierced through the city with some frequency, as Hester relays to Val:

The siren has just gone again – we have at least one almost every night now. They don't usually seem to lead to anything much, though you sometimes hear a crump or two in the distance, I'm thankful to say. But they do give one that peculiar feeling inside still – in fact it's unsettling in every sense of the word!

The war also brought with it a scarcity of consumer goods. Food was rationed and specific items were hard to come by, but clothing was also rationed on a points-based system from 1st June 1941, with different articles of clothing costing different amounts of coupons. The huge demand for military uniform and the disruption to the supply chain of both materials and finished goods meant the clothing industry was stretched thin. Even when one had the coupons, it was sometimes difficult to find the necessary items in the right sizes, as Hester found out:

I have been trying to buy some shoes & an odd skirt (navy blue, for the office) which you wouldn't think was very difficult, but I find it quite impossible to get anything wearable! If I took size three or size eight in shoes I should have no trouble at all but as my feet are a medium size there's no hope for me.

It seemed that she had the seven coupons to spare for a skirt and a second five for a pair of women's shoes, plus the money to pay for them, but that meant nothing if the items weren't available. The Make Do and Mend campaign wasn't just something women adopted to support the war effort, it was a necessity in the face of clothing shortages.

When Christmas came around, things were even more difficult. The customary present buying meant demands were even higher, and supplies just couldn't keep up:

Everyone is just beginning to pour into the shops to do their Christmas shopping, and one has to do it very early before they're completely stripped. There is very little to buy anyway – I have been trying to get a pair of black suede gloves for Mother for about a month, and can't find any possible ones in the whole of London.

One of the ways clothes rationing could be circumvented was by the bringing back or sending of clothing from abroad. With the international movement of troops, this was an option for some women and Hester appeared to have been hoping, in vain, that she might be treated to a French luxury as a birthday or Christmas present:

After reading what you say in your letter about the prices in Paris, I feel that it must have seemed horrid of me to have mentioned stockings and scent in my last letter, when you had just sent me such a generous present. I do hope you didn't think that – it was only that I do sometimes long for something French – gayer and more amusing than the English things, and above all, different! It is probably very selfish to think like this at all, but the dead level of monotony in one's daily life in the last five years does sometimes make one hunger for the unattainable!

Hester seems to have been particularly fond of Paris. After four years of Nazi occupation, the liberation of Paris was won after a six-day battle that ended when the French capital was finally surrendered. The initial plan by Allied forces had been to bypass the city as they pushed German forces out of France, not wanting to engage in a difficult urban battle, but the French people were unwilling to allow their city to stay in German hands.

French Resistance fighters began an uprising, starting with strikes across the city. With order destabilised and amid concerns that a communist faction might liberate

Paris and prevent a democratic government from being re-established, Allied troops moved in to assist. The French 2nd Armoured Division and the U.S. 4th Infantry Division liberated the city with relative ease, with many German troops surrendering or fleeing. Thankfully, Hitler's order to blow up Paris' landmarks and burn it to the ground if the Allies made a move to retake the city was not carried out.

This was the Paris that Val experienced, and the one he wrote to Hester of. Her reply makes it clear she cared for the city:

My very best thanks to you for your masterly account of liberated Paris! It is so detailed & seemed to cover all the things I wanted to know, even fashions! & how the Parisians have emerged from the last four years. But what you told me depresses me, too. It's such a desolate scene you describe – I wonder if Paris will ever return to her old smart, gay, fascinating self again. She MUST. If she does not, it will be a very great tragedy, not only for France, but for the whole world. But she will, when times are better. I'm certain.

The monotony of war, after so many years, was starting to take its toll, but Hester and Val's letters span a duration that includes Victory in Europe Day on 8th May 1945, which saw the official end of the war in Europe. Val was keen to hear of the celebrations back in Britain, as he would remain in France for some time, and urged Hester to speak of the scenes in London. She was rather hesitant, but did eventually relent:

> I'll only say that, after the disappointment of Monday that followed the endless rumours that Churchill was going to broadcast at any minute now, a good time was had by all – slightly tempered by the fact that a good many people were feeling rather tired & rather sad, & remembering that although one war was over, the second was still very much on. However it was all great fun, & Churchill was cheered to the echo whenever he appeared. There were no church bells that I could hear, no fountains & no bands, except one rather small band in Whitehall at one point, but there were plenty of bonfires & the floodlighting in St. James's Park was rather good.

The majority of the letters included in the box concern life before peace in Europe, so any mentions of the rebuilding of the country and the slow return to normal life are few and far between, but Hester did mention, while reporting on a trip with her mother, that 'They have opened part of the beaches at Brighton & Hove, but some parts are still being cleared of wires'.

Amid concerns that Brighton might be the site of a sea-borne invasion, the beaches had been closed in July 1940, after the surrender of France and the British retreat from Dunkirk left the town a potential target. The beaches were subsequently lined with land mines and barbed wire was set up both to make things harder for the enemy if they landed, and to keep British civilians away from the mines. The Palace Pier, now usually known as just Brighton Pier, and the West Pier, then still in working order, had decking removed so they couldn't be used by any invading forces as landing docks. Gun crews stationed near the shore were given the instruction to destroy the piers if necessary, to prevent them being used in an invasion.

Hester and her mother's visit so soon after the war that defences were still being removed demonstrates how keen the British people were to return to normality, including holidaying by the sea.

As with any relationship, Hester and Val were not without their disputes. Drafts of letters containing arguments are unlikely to be the ones you would be most likely to keep, so the scale of any friction between them is hard to say, but one practise letter regarding a visit to see Hester's lifelong friend Esme Greig, nee Langton, did survive in the box:

Darling, please don't be cross & difficult about this. I really can't put Esme off, I haven't been down to see them for ages, though she has asked me in nearly every letter, & if I didn't go this time I know she would be hurt – & as she is one of my best friends I can't allow that to happen. [...]

And now what about lunch tomorrow? If you are going to talk to me in that hard, distant voice you spoke in on the telephone this morning I don't feel I can bear it. I've never heard you speak like that before. It didn't sound like you at all.

It's nice to see Hester's devotion to her friendship and, despite Val's apparent annoyance that she would put visiting Esme before seeing him, they seem to have moved past this grievance. We are not entirely sure exactly when the relationship between Val and Hester ended, or exactly why. The best theory that can be drawn from the letters Hester preserved is perhaps that she was desiring a marriage to Val, and he was unable or unwilling to pursue it.

Divorce was possible at this time, but not easy, as seen in the case of Hester's brother, Donald, but Val's wife would have had more than enough to support a petition for divorce on the grounds of adultery. What might perhaps be the last of the letters in the box is one we can date between 8th May 1945 and 2nd September 1945, owing to Hester's specification that the war was over 'here', but peace had not entirely been achieved. In this letter, Hester talked rather vaguely, but her words can be read as a desire to formalise their relationship, something it seems she had promised to put off until after the war but could no longer ignore:

It's fairly easy for you to cope with these things, but of course it's quite difficult for me & my dear I think we

must try & do something about it as soon as possible.
Now the war here is over & I have kept my promise to not
say anything more about it till then, though it has often
been very difficult in many ways. I do wish I could see
you & talk things over – letters are most unsatisfactory
for anything of this sort, & it sometimes takes so long to
get an answer. But I can't go on like this much longer, so
do write to me as soon as you can & tell me that you are
making some plans for us. I would so much rather that
the subject had been raised again by you than me – but I
think you will understand.

One of the lines from the song *Dear Bill* in the musical
is taken almost directly from Hester's 'Pam' letters: 'Why
did we meet in the middle of a war? What a silly thing for
anyone to do.' One has to wonder whether, if Hester felt
like the war was preventing her relationship with Val from
progressing, that line came from somewhere very personal.

Not a huge amount about the rest of Val's life is known.
He lived at 130 Queens Gate in Kensington from 1945
to 1947, with a man named John Fullerton Evetts, and in
1966 he was fined £15 for careless driving, at which point
he was living at 74 Pennington Road, Southborough.
When he died, on 30th November 1975, his will, written
in 1960, revealed that he had left everything to his wife,
Inez. It is unclear whether they had reconciled and begun
their relationship again, or whether he simply had no one
else to leave it to, having no children of his own.

The final thing that gives Val a place in the Operation Mincemeat story is his inclusion amongst the ranks of those who have been incorrectly remembered owing to a mistaken name. Cecil Liddell, a member of B1H., once referred to him as Victor, an error that is still included in contemporary books about World War Two.

The letters and diaries that the Leggatt family so generously allowed us to take a look at were the final pieces of the puzzle that demolished the myth of Hester as an antagonistic old spinster who had never experienced love. They provided us a look at Hester that we never expected to see, giving her depth and humour that only endeared her to us further.

CONCLUSION

SOON THE JOURNEY WILL BE DONE

HISTORICAL wills have found themselves in the news lately as the Ministry of Justice announced they were considering a plan to digitise all post-1858 wills and then destroy the originals, citing an effort to cut down on storage costs as the reason for the controversial move. It was not taken well by many archivists, historians and researchers, who called attention to the risks that come with relying solely on digital storage.

Scanning errors would be inevitable when bearing in mind the scale of the project, with about 100 million wills being considered for the bin. With no originals to turn back to, blurred, cut off or otherwise imperfect scans would simply result in a loss of information. Once scanned and stored away on a server, those digital files would still be at risk of degrading, being hacked, and of human error that could see them deleted and unrecoverable. Without physical, securely stored originals as backups, it would be taking a huge level of risk with this historical material.

One of the efforts to convince the public of the upsides to this cost-saving measure was to reassure people that the wills of famous people would be kept, but a decision of who was famous enough to be saved is never going to be an unbiased one. There might be universal agreement on some names, with media suggesting that Charles Darwin, Charles Dickens and Diana, Princess of Wales would all make the cut, but someone can be hugely famous and influential in their field but relatively unknown to the wider public. Some people, like Hester, might die after a life that seemed fairly ordinary and not be recognised for something significant until much later. Hester Leggatt is not the only person out there who needs finding.

It wasn't until towards the end of our Hester research that we turned to her will, but that turned out to be the perfect time to do it. After all the investigating we had done, so much of it made immediate sense and connected to things we had already learnt. Hester initially made her will in September 1982 and subsequently wrote three codicils, providing her address each time and thus allowing us to confirm where she had been living towards the end of her life. She stayed in London until her early 90s, at which point she moved into a nursing home in Goring-on-Thames, and then to Chilton House, a care home in Chilton.

Many of the names on Hester's will are people with no real personal connection to her life. There are a few solicitors acting in a professional capacity and the witnesses seem to be employees at a solicitor's office, or staff at the care homes Hester was living at. It is amongst the beneficiaries, however, where the personal links can be found.

Hester bequeaths her 'Cousin' Sheana Strachan her sapphire and diamond ring. We, of course, did a little more family history research and discovered that Sheana was Hester's second cousin once removed, born in 1915 and seemingly spending much of her early life in India, similar to Hester. She worked for the Women's Auxiliary Territorial Service in World War Two, before working in the Foreign Office for the rest of her career, being made an MBE in 1960. She died unmarried in 1999, four years after Hester. What happened to Hester's sapphire and diamond ring at that point is unknown.

Hester also left £300 to Colin Greig, who she identifies as her godson. Colin, who had been born in 1929, was Esme and Geoffrey Greig's son. Hester and Esme's friendship lasted their entire lives. They seemingly met as children; Hester attended Esme's wedding; she had been, as the will showed, godmother to at least one of her children and the pair were still friends until Esme died in 1994. As she pre-deceased Hester, she would never be a beneficiary of Hester's will, but she would have been allocated one item of her choosing not otherwise disposed of, suggesting she had no need for money, but that Hester still wanted to provide something sentimental to recognise their friendship.

The same gesture of sentiment was made to Allison Dorothea Lynes, nee Waller. Allison also had childhood links to India, born in 1905 to the sister of the Viceroy. Many of the addresses we could find for her throughout her life place her near Hester. It is possible that she is the Allison mentioned in Hester's diary as one of the many people she organised social events with, but she is certainly the Allison mentioned in a letter in which Hester told Val 'On Saturday I am going on to Littlehampton for a few days to stay with Allison & Charles Lynes', proving her indeed to be another long-standing friend. Allison Lynes also pre-deceased Hester, so would never receive the bequest.

The original chief beneficiary of Hester's will was Katherine Eleanor Prain, who Hester identified as 'my dear Cousin [...] who has been so good to me.' Katherine was the daughter of Victoria Eleanor Murray, the sister of Hester's mother, and she and Hester seem to have been close throughout their lives. She is potentially the Katherine that Hester notes having coffee with in her wartime diaries. They often lived very near each other and, in 1992, were both living together at 17 Lennox Gardens. They would live at the same nursing home in their final years and when Katherine passed away in January 1994, she left Hester all her 'clothes wearing apparel furs and fur coats.'

Hester also set aside £3,000 to repay a personal loan from Connel Leggatt, wife of her brother Bill. She specified that this was 'in repayment of the interest free loan made to me so kindly some years ago,' but does not provide the detail of exactly when the money was originally loaned. It seems likely, though, that Hester is not referring to a time that stretched back as far as 1946, when Bill passed away, so we can assume that Hester and Connel remained in touch after this point, with Hester getting to spend time with her nieces and nephews. They would be the ones to receive the £3,000, split between them in line with the terms of Hester's will, as Connel predeceased Hester in 1988.

Everything that remained of Hester's estate after these bequests was to be liquidated and used to pay for her funeral and any outstanding debts. Initially, the remaining amount was to be split equally between Donald Patrick Leggatt and a series of charities. Donald was Hester's nephew and godson, son of her brother Donald who had passed away in 1942. Later, Hester would change her will to leave half of her remaining estates to be divided in this way, and the other half to anyone else she had requested in other papers, which are not known to have survived if they ever existed.

Hester's choice of charities varied throughout the original will and the codicils, but began as the Marie Curie Memorial Foundation, initially dedicated to caring for people with cancer but now a broader end of life charity for people with any terminal illness; The National Trust and The National Trust for Scotland, both natural and cultural conservation charities; and The Distressed Gentlefolk's Aid Association, now known at Turn2us, which assists those who have fallen on hard times.

Hester later changed the charities to The Samaritans, the suicide prevention charity that the British Council would donate to in her name after her death; The Salvation Army, a church that carries out community-based charity work; and Shelter, a homelessness and housing charity.

The final codicil, which specifies these last three charities, was made just over a month before Hester passed away. It seemed she was aware she was near the end of her life and wanted to make sure her money would go to the charities that mattered most to her. She died at the Chilton House care home on the 26th July 1995. In accordance with her will, her body was cremated and her ashes were scattered. This would explain why, back in 2021, there was no listing for her headstone on the Find a Grave website that had started one researcher's interest in the real lives of the *Operation Mincemeat* musical's characters.

Hester's will reveals a series of lifetime friendships and enduring connections with the families of both of her brothers, despite their early deaths, something that was confirmed by her great-niece when we made contact with her towards the end of our research. She remembers meeting Hester, although knew nothing of her war work. She recalls Hester as tall and forbidding, with an extremely upper-class voice. When Hester gifted the family a box of chocolates every year, they seemed to be a regift of something Hester herself had received the year before. Hester also visited the family for tea from time to time, an occasion that called for the silver teapot to be set out.

Hester's great-niece also remembers Hester's friendship with Katherine Prain. The two were taken to tea by Hester's nephew near the BBC, where he worked, and would accompany each other to weddings.

Banish the thought of her being a lonely old spinster. Every document we have discovered showed Hester to be incredibly social, with a wide network of friends. We got to experience her humour, her frustrations, her love and how much she cared deeply about those who mattered to her. It was more than we ever expected would be out there, surviving decades and waiting to be found.

It is impossible to say that we've learnt everything there is to know about Hester, and in many ways, we hope there is more to come. We still have alerts set up on online auction websites on the off chance that someone else decides to sell another book inscribed to her. Archive collections are continually being catalogued and digitised, becoming widely available in ways they have never been before and allowing for links to be identified between pieces of material. Ten years ago, the work we did would have been considerably harder, not least because we would likely never have met and pooled our resources. What we have achieved, however, is a more detailed picture of who Hester was than we could have ever imagined. We are thrilled to have been able to discover her story, and to tell it, and we are delighted that the *Operation Mincemeat* musical has embraced our research so enthusiastically.

The story of Operation Mincemeat seems to be cursed to carry with it inaccuracies and mistakes in books, articles, documentaries and any other form of media that features it. It even continues into media about the musical now, with articles continually getting things wrong regarding the writers, the actors or the show itself. Perhaps it is simply a matter of us now knowing far too much about the musical and having accidently become Hester Leggatt experts, and the errors on these subjects specifically stick out to us. Maybe every book and article out there is wrong at least once, and we just don't have the knowledge to pick up on it. We have of course, tried our best with this book, because Hester deserves nothing less, but given the curse of Mincemeat mistakes, really who knows.

Operation Mincemeat is still running at the Fortune Theatre in London, with the baton of portraying Hester passed from Jak Malone to Christian Andrews in May 2024. It's a two-sided experience for Jak to watch someone else play her, part protectiveness over his own version of the character, and part quiet satisfaction that Hester is still there, night after night, telling her story and writing her love letter regardless of whether he is there to supervise. Not that he could stay away for too long – he helped open the show on Broadway, reprising the role of Hester once again.

Jak's portrayal of Hester didn't change after the research, with SpitLip's Hester an entirely separate entity from the real Hester we uncovered. She had been created over multiple runs of the show and many years and had an entirely different backstory, and adapting her at that point wasn't really possible, or what anyone wanted. None of the other characters in the show were exact replicas of their real inspirations anyway. So, while the spelling of Hester's name was changed in the programme, the Hester you see on stage is still the same as from before the research began.

In April 2024, Jak won an Olivier Award, the most well-known and prestigious theatre awards in the UK, for his portrayal of Hester in *Operation Mincemeat*. Winning the award is an accomplishment in itself, but there was an extra level of joy for Jak to have received it specifically for playing Hester. Hester got her plaque at the Fortune Theatre because Jak's performance moved us to research her, and Jak got his award for playing her. It seemed a fair trade. Although he does think that the real Hester would rather hate the show. We're not so sure. She liked the theatre, and her letters revealed an excellent sense of humour, so perhaps *Operation Mincemeat* would have won her over.

The musical ends with a moment to pause and reflect on Glyndwr Michael, the real identity of the man whose corpse was used in the operation. The audience is reminded that we tend to focus on men like the fictional William Martin, forgetting the people that worked behind him and the importance of their stories. The cast use their natural accents as they share the little we know about Glyndwr Michael. He was born in Wales and worked as a gardener and general labourer. He made his way to London, with no remaining family, where he found himself homeless until his death.

He died of poisoning after eating bread crusts smeared with rat poison. It is unclear whether this was an intentional act at the end of a desperate life, or if Michael was simply hungry and had not realised that the bread was intended as rat bait. Hester likely never knew the exact circumstances of how Major William Martin's body was obtained, so her financial support of Samaritans and Shelter in her will is just the last serendipitous coincidence in this story, with her bequests going on to help prevent suicide and help those experiencing homelessness.

The show goes on to draw attention to the change made to William Martin's headstone in Huelva in 1998, with the addition of the inscription 'Glyndwr Michael Served as Major William Martin, RM'. The identification of the body was made possible by amateur historian Roger Morgan who, two years earlier, had found an accidental, uncensored instance of Glyndwr Michael's name in official paperwork.

There is a long history of returning people's names and identities to them when it comes to the Operation Mincemeat story. Ewen Montagu couldn't let Charles Cholmondeley's death pass by without publicly recognising his efforts during the war and the lives he saved as a result. Roger Morgan discovered the long-buried identity of Glyndwr Michael, allowing him to finally be commemorated for the unwitting part he played in MI5's deception efforts. We are honoured to be able to do the same for Hester, and for Averil. When we talk about Operation Mincemeat, we ought to include their names, correctly spelt.

ACKNOWLEDGEMENTS

THIS entire endeavour has been a group project from the start, so it's perhaps inevitable that the list of people we need to acknowledge is a long one. Please do bear with us.

We owe a huge amount of gratitude to Andrew Lownie for believing we could turn this wild little story into a book that other people might want to read, and to Clare, Claire, Jo, Christine and everyone at Mirror Books who kept that belief going and got this book into your hands.

Hester's living relatives have shown us incredible support and took being thrown into the middle of the mad world that is Operation Mincemeat incredibly well. Their trust in providing us with Hester's diaries and letters remains one of the most touching parts of this entire process for us. It has been an honour to tell her story.

We also have to thank the Montagu family, for putting up with our weird and specific questions. To Saul, especially, for fielding said questions and for his friendship, and to Sarah, for the answers.

Dr Philip Milln was also very generous with his time and his mother's memories, and we are very grateful for the trust he showed us in sharing Averil's story.

We are also very grateful to the staff at Wycombe Abbey, Charterhouse and Winchester for answering our questions about Hester and her brothers. Lauren Nguy and Jesús Copeiro were great help with the research into William Watkins. Similarly, those we interacted with at Keble College, Bletchley Park, the British Council, University of Reading, the Imperial War Museum and the National Archives all helped immensely. The National Archives are an immensely valuable public resource that everyone should consider visiting. Whether writing a thesis or pursuing a passion project, the records they hold are an incredible glimpse into the history of this country.

Celia Dugan and Ben Macintyre have been supportive of the quest to find Hester throughout its many twists and turns and gone above and beyond to put Hester's name on plaques and in newspapers, respectively.

Without the *Operation Mincemeat* musical, we would probably never have known there was a Hester to find. We therefore have to thank SpitLip for their incredible show, as well as the equally incredible support they have shown us during the research efforts and book writing. Additionally, David, Natasha and Zoë, along with Christian, Claire, Geri, Holly, Jak and Seán, brought all these characters to life in a way that gave us no choice but to connect with them. We fell in love with them because of the way you portrayed them, so we would never have found Hester without you all.

ACKNOWLEDGEMENTS

A huge additional thank you to Jak for saying yes to everything when it came to this entire project, be it interviews or bookmark-drawing or foreword-writing, even while moving countries and rehearsing for a Broadway show. It means so much that you always found the time.

You can find the names of the Finding Hester researchers on Hester's plaque at the Fortune Theatre, but for the sake of calling attention to them and their contributions to this mission, we want to record them here as well. Our thanks therefore goes to Annabel Rose, Ben Caligari, Bram de Buyser, Caitlin DeAngelis, Elinor Quick, Gail Bishop, Hûw Steer, Jan Schneider, Jenny Murray, Jessie Honnor, Kathy Bolt, Maayan Shir, Misha Anker, Philippa Peall, Rachel Pantrey, Sarah Haynes, Sharon O'Connor, Silvia Lemos, Sophie Message and Valeria Oliveira.

Annabel is much deserving of additional thanks for her contribution to the book, and for her unending support throughout the writing process. Jan and Sharon were also hugely helpful as we pulled all the research together into something cohesive. The book would not exist without the three of you.

And a final thank you to all the Mincefluencers, whether you helped in the quest to find Hester directly, or you cheered from the sidelines.

Despite it being at odds with our entire goal of finding someone history might have forgotten, we have almost inevitably forgotten someone here. All we can offer is our apologies, and the hope that the act of returning to Hester her name and her story is a fitting acknowledgment of all the many people who helped make it happen. If it's up, it's up as one.

Ewen Montague on right and Charles Cholmondeley on 17th April 1943 while transporting the body to Scotland

A photograph of MI5 worker Jean Leslie at the beach, used as the face of 'Pam', the pilot's fictitious fiancée

Barry House 1922 photograph, featuring girls in positions of responsibility within the house. We believe Hester is third from the left, seated.

WEDDING COINCIDENCE.—Mr. Geoffrey G. Greig, son of the Bishop of Guildford, with his bride, Miss Esme Langton, after their wedding, the first in the New Charterhouse Chapel. The bride's mother was the first bride at the Old Charterhouse Chapel.

Geoffrey and Esme Greig's wedding, as reported in the *Daily Mirror* on 1st August 1928. Hester is likely the adult bridesmaid behind the two young trainbearers.

WEDDING OF BISHOP OF GUILDFORD'S SON.—The marriage of Mr. G. G. F. Greig to Miss Esmé Langton was the to be solemnised in the fine new Chapel at Charterhouse.

Esme and Geoffrey's wedding. It's from *The Surrey Advertiser* on 4th August 1928. Hester is stood directly to the right of the bride

Hester Leggatt's plaque in the lobby at the Fortune Theatre

Averil Gurdon on her wedding day

Milln — Gurdon

Lt. Anthony David Milln, R.N., youngest son of the late Surg.-Capt. J. D. S. Milln, R.N., and of Mrs. Milln, of Alverstoke, Hants., married Miss Averil Elizabeth Gurdon, elder daughter of Major-Gen. and Mrs. E. T. L. Gurdon, of Burgh House, near Woodbridge, at St. Mary's, Grundisburgh, Suffolk

Jak Malone in costume as Hester backstage of the *Operation Mincemeat* musical

1915

William Leggatt's 1915 house photograph at Winchester College. His surname is misspelt 'Leggett' in the caption

MISS IRIS SOLOMON AND THE HON. EWEN MONTAGU

Whose wedding is fixed to take place on June 14. Miss Solomon is the younger daughter of the famous artist, Mr. Solomon J. Solomon, P.R.B.A., R.A., and Mrs. Solomon. Mr. Ewen Montagu is Lord Swaythling's second son

Ewen Montagu in the 1919 Westminster School whole school photograph

Ewen Montagu, his fiancée Iris, and Pip the dog

The Charterhouse School Football 1st XI from the 1915-16 season. Hester's brother Donald is on the righthand side of the seated row

Naval identity card of Major Martin with photograph of Captain Ronnie Reed (above)

Hester's wartime love letters to Val

3rd November 1944

Three letters of yours to answer, darling! — let's call it two and half, as one was the short one about the newspapers. And they all arrived within just over 24 hours, though the first one is dated the 22nd and the last the 29th. Now I'll do you a list to show you how queer it all is :—

Date	Portsmouth	Arrived
a) 22nd	25th	1st
b) 27th	28th	1st
c) 29th	31st	2nd

So you see the first one was postmarked three days after the date of the letter. And before that, I had been without one for nine days. Though I love getting letters I do wish same—

A draft letter from Hester
13th October 1944

272

'Pam''s letters, included in the Operation Mincemeat briefcase, written by Hester

William Watkins in the centre of the group of women *(top)*;
Group photo with Watkins in the centre of the middle row and
Francis Haselden on the far left of the same row

Watkins' draft card *(left)*; A memo
in Montagu's papers signed 'HL'
in Hester's handwriting *(right)*

SOURCES

ARCHIVES:

Canford School Archive, Canford
Charterhouse School Archive, Godalming
Imperial War Museum Collections, London
Keble College Archive, Oxford
The British Library, London
The National Archives, Kew (TNA)
University of Reading Archive, Reading
Westminster School Archive, London
Winchester College Archive, Winchester
Wycombe Abbey Archive, Wycombe

NEWSPAPERS AND JOURNALS:

After the Battle
Baltimore Sun
Boston Globe
Daily Mirror
Daily Telegraph
Exeter and Plymouth Gazette
Homeward Mail from India, China and the East
London Gazette
New York Times

San Antonio Express News
Surrey Advertiser
Surrey Times
West Surrey Times
West Sussex Gazette
Western Times

INTERVIEWS:

Jak Malone, actor in Operation Mincemeat musical. Video interview with the author: 16th August 2024.

Jak Malone, actor in Operation Mincemeat musical. Correspondence with the author: 29th September 2024.

Jesus Copéiro, author. Correspondence with the author: 20 August 2023 and 10 December 2024

BOOKS AND ARTICLES:

Borreguero Beltrán, Julia M. "El hombre que nunca existió" o el espionaje alemán en Huelva durante la segunda guerra mundial in *mAGAzin* issue 2, 1997.

FitzGerald, Desmond. *Many Parts: The Life and Travels of a Soldier, Engineer, and Arbitrator in Africa and Beyond*, Palgrave Macmillan, 2007.

Goold Walker, G. *The Honourable Artillery Company, 1537–1987*, Honourable Artillery Company, 1986.

Smyth, Denis. *Deathly Deception: The Real Story of Operation Mincemeat*, Oxford University Press, 2010.

Macintyre, Ben. *Operation Mincemeat: The True Spy Story*

That Changed the Course of World War Two, Bloomsbury, 2010.

McCrery, Nigel. *The Coming Storm: Test and First-Class Cricketers Killed in World War Two*, Pen & Sword Books, 2017.

Montagu, Ewen. Beyond Top Secret U, Coward, McCann & Geoghegan, 1978 [1977].

Montagu, Ewen. *The Man Who Never Was Man Who Never Was*: The Remarkable Story of Operation Mincemeat, The History Press, 2021 [1953].

Montagu, Ivor. *The Youngest Son: Autobiographical Chapters*, Lawrence & Wishart, 1970.

Morrison, James. *The Journal Of James Morrison Boatswain's Mate Of The Bounty Describing The Mutiny And Subsequent Misfortunes Of The Mutineers Together With An Account Of The Island Of Tahiti*, The Golden Cockerel Press, 1935.

Nielsen-Hidalgo Vigo, Enrique and Ramírez Copeiro del Villar, Jesús. William Martin. *Operación Carne Picada*, Editorial Niebla, 2018.

Vernon, Robert W. "Beyond Huelva: Other British Mining Legacies in Andalucia, Spain" in *Proceedings of the 6th International Mining History Congress*, Akabira, Hokkaido, Japan, 2003.

Ziegler, Philip. *Osbert Sitwell*, Chatto & Windus, 1998.

ONLINE:

abhilekh-patal.in

ancestry.com

ata-ferry-pilots.org

bletchleypark.org.uk

britishnewspaperarchive.co.uk

bucksgardentrust.org.uk

canford.com

charterhouse.org.uk

chilternscrematorium.co.uk

christies.com

collections.westminster.org.uk

digital.nls.uk

findmypast.co.uk

freebmd.org.uk

layersoflondon.org

myheritage.com

roll-of-honour.com

twitter.com

USCensus.com

winchestercollege.org

wycombeabbey.com

familysearch.org

CHAPTER NOTES

CHAPTER ONE:

'In her interview' Macintyre, Operation Mincemeat, 2010, p. 77

'When Jak listens back to it' Malone video interview, 16 Aug 2024

'When Jak took Hester on' Ibid

'Jak sometimes regretted his decision' Ibid

'Jak remembers the rehearsal process' Ibid

'Jak Malone will admit' Ibid

CHAPTER TWO:

'Really sadly we could find' SpitLip tweet 11 Jun 2023

CHAPTER THREE:

'The census shows Hester as a fifteen-year-old school-girl' 1921 United Kingdom Census via ancestry.com

'Hester attended Wycombe Abbey' Ibid

'Charterhouse' Ibid

Winchester College' Winchester College Roll of Honour

'Even on the same page of the 1921 Census form' 1921 United Kingdom Census via ancestry.com 'both brothers were boarding at the Parkside School' 1911 United Kingdom Census via ancestry.com

'the British India Office Birth and Baptism records' India, Select Births and Baptisms 1786-1947 via ancestry.com

'Her father was born in 1870' myheritage.com

'her mother was born in Bombay in 1874' Ibid

'Jessie Leggatt was one of four children' Ibid

'In the 1901 Census, she is living in Notting Hill' 1901 United Kingdom Census via ancestry.com

'Hester passed away 4th August 1995' National Private Calendar via ancestry.com

'our timeline of Hester's life positioned her in Kensington' Kensington and Chelsea Electoral Registers via ancestry.com

FINDING CHARLES:

'Cholmondeley's father was Eton educated' Email correspondence with family

'When he attended school in England' https://www.ata-ferry-pilots.org/index.php/component/tags/tag/australian-pilots

'From at least as early as 1941, he resided' Ibid

'No bomb damage is recorded' https://www.layersoflondon.org/map/overlays/bomb-damage-1945

'He attended Canford School' Canford School Archive

'he won the third form mathematics prize' The Canfordian, Canford School Archive

'His first year at the School coincided' Ibid

'serving as secretary' Ibid

'would return as an Old Canfordian' Ibid

'he would actually go on to study geography' Keble College Archive

'He joined the college on the 9th October' Ibid

'he played in the College hockey team' Ibid

'sat an Agriculture prelim' Ibid

'once the war had come to an end' Ibid

'took up a job as a First Locust Officer' TNA FO 957/28

'a report on the 1948 activities' Ibid

CHAPTER FOUR:

'Hester took the Royal Academy of Music' West Surrey Times, 19 Jan 1917

'pass the Elementary division' Surrey Times, 4 May 1918

'use a School Roll to confirm Hester's enrolment' Wycombe Abbey Archive

'mentioned in the list of new girls' Wycombe Abbey Archive The Gazette

'1922 issue of the magazine' Ibid

'Confirmed in December 1921' Ibid

'a report of 'an Entertainment'' Ibid

'In Hester's own handwriting' Wycombe Abbey Archive

Senior Roll book

'September 1949 Certificate of Registration' TNA HO 334/446/1437

'short entries to keep up with their alumni' Wycombe Abbey Archive

'walked in the procession to the chapel' Surrey Advertiser, 4 Aug 1928, via British Newspaper Archive

FINDING EWEN:

'When Montagu's wife and two young children returned' Email correspondence with family

'were considered half-boarders' Westminster School Archive

'having come down with 'German measles'' Ibid

'His older brother had left the School' Ibid

'Contemporary pupils recalled a Zeppelin raid' Westminster School Archive WS/02/HOU/04/01/01

'The chess ledger revealed' Westminster School Archive WS/02/SOC/09/01

'took part in the Rigaud's Literary Society's reading' Westminster School Archive WS/02/HOU/04/01/01

'spent a three week stint at a Harvest Camp' Ibid

'One of the cast members does remember it' Malone video interview, 16 Aug 2024

'That was Pip' Email correspondence with family

'a fair menagerie of animals' Montagu, Ivor, The Youngest Son, 1970, p. 68

'We are glad to see that Montagu' Westminster School Archive WS/02/PUB/01/05/430

'Montagu had trained as an instructor' Email correspondence with family

'He recalled his classics being poor' Unpublished autobiography by Ewen Montagu, shared by family

CHAPTER FIVE:

'Donald's time at Charterhouse' Charterhouse School Archive

'In 1917 he joined the Royal Navy' 1918 Navy List via National Library of Scotland GAB.16, p. 188

'his knowledge was below the usual standard' TNA ADM 196/148/23 p.23

'married Valerie Edith Rose De Mattos' Western Times, 12 Jan 1923 via British Newspaper Archive

'Valerie cited that her request for a divorce' TNA J77/3356/2464

'Donald remarried' 1935 Marriage records via ancestry. com

'Donald re-joined the Navy' Charterhouse School Memorial Chapel roll of honour via roll-of-honour

'a telegram was sent to the Admiralty' TNA ADM 358/980

'boarding in Du Boulay's house' Winchester College Archive

'played a game of football against Westminster School'

Westminster School Archive

'an avid and prolific writer of letters' Winchester College Society newspaper The Trusty Servant No. 117 May 2014

'William stayed with the army between the wars' TNA WO 373/23/279

'first guns ashore in the invasion of Sicily' Goold Walker, The Honourable Artillery Company, 1537–1987, 1986, p. 315.

'suffered a heart attack' Citizen, 14th August 1946, via ancestry.com

'moved from the accommodation they'd shared' Kensington Electoral Register via ancestry.com

CHAPTER SIX:

Historians have spelt Leggatt incorrectly' Email correspondence with family

'being amazed, excited and strangely proud' Ibid

'It was great to meet the team' Ibid

FINDING HASELDEN

'In the La Caroline area' Vernon, "Beyond Huelva", 2003

'The network also fulfilled an important anti-sabotage role' Borreguero Beltrán, "El hombre que nunca existió", 1997

'activities ran primarily out of Haselden's own house' Nielsen-Hidalgo Vigo and Ramírez Copeiro del Villar.

William Martin. Operación Carne Picada, 2018

'Sinclair also took over as' Ibid

'Even Haselden's close accomplices in counterespionage' Borreguero Beltrán, "El hombre que nunca existió", 1997

'Haselden was instructed to make enquiries' Macintyre, Operation Mincemeat, 2010, ch. 15

'Lt Pascual del Pobil then offered the documents' Ibid

'earning the ire of the local British community' Nielsen-Hidalgo Vigo and Ramírez Copeiro del Villar. William Martin. Operación Carne Picada, 2018

'encourage the interception of the documents by Adolf Clauss' Macintyre, Operation Mincemeat, 2010, ch. 15

'British consulate then contracted to pay' Macintyre, Operation Mincemeat, 2010, ch. 17

'Haselden then passed on this information' Ibid

'first at Broadway and then at Bletchley Park' Bletchley Park roll of Honour via bletchleypark.org.uk

CHAPTER SEVEN:

'the 1915 caption had his name' Winchester College Archive

CHAPTER EIGHT:

'two of these letters' University of Reading MS 1979/7/1

'inscribed a copy of Brighton' Correspondence with Beaux Books, Hampshire

'A lot of three books relating to Golden Cockerel Press' Christie's lot 4347535

'he praises the work of 'Miss Hester Leggatt' Morrison, James. The Journal Of James Morrison, 1935 via The British Library

'discovered a letter written by Maynard Hollingworth' Ziegler, Osbert Sitwell, 1998, p. 234

'a letter from the British Council' Private correspondence with British Council provided by the Leggatt family

'Hester's personnel file has either been destroyed or lost' Private correspondence with British Council

'Hester May Murray Leggatt has worked at MI5' Private correspondence with MI5

FINDING AVERIL

'None of us had felt up to writing the letters' Montagu, The Man Who Never Was Man Who Never Was, 1953

'Charles Cholmondeley's date for the evening' Macintyre, Operation Mincemeat, 2010, p. 185

CHAPTER NINE:

'it was all a little overwhelming at first' Malone video interview, 16 Aug 2024

'he had a strange connection to Hester' Ibid

'We were captivated by the mystery of Hester Leggatt' Operation Mincemeat programme, second printing, August 2032

'Art doesn't change things' Hodgson live speech at Fortune Theatre 11th December 2023

'Hester herself would be very gratified' Leggatt live speech at Fortune Theatre 11th December 2023

'the fully realised, wonderful woman' Malone live speech at Fortune Theatre 11th December 2023

FINDING WATKINS

'larger than life' Malone correspondence, 29th September 2024

'Three days before the body' Macintyre, Operation Mincemeat, 2010, p. 198

'He lost three brothers in World War Two' San Antonio Express News, "Tarleton Watkins Obituary", 2009

'They had five sons' 1920 United States Census

'Ruth Harvin married' The Boston Globe, Ruth Watkins Obituary

'signed up for that first induction' John Chester Anderson Watkins Draft Card

'He wasn't shot up' Baltimore Sun, "Veteran Airman…"

'I was a fisherman' Nielsen-Hidalgo Vigo and Ramírez Copeiro del Villar. William Martin. Operación Carne Picada, 2018

'My father had to be aware' Ibid

'He crashed in Spain one day' Baltimore Sun, "Veteran Airman…"

"Early in 1943 he was forced down in Spain' Baltimore

Sun, "Aviation Editor Is Home With Medals" 17th February 1944

'his body was repatriated from Bari, Italy' William Anderson Watkins interment card

CHAPTER TEN:

Quotations from private collection of Hester's diaries and letters

CHAPTER ELEVEN:

'born on 25th January 1982' TNA HO 334/62

'naturalised as a British citizen in 1914' Ibid

'living at 21 Sandyford Place' Ibid

Quotations from private collection of Hester's diaries and letters

CONCLUSION

'worked for the Women's Auxiliary Territorial Service' *The Gazette* via ancestry.com

'made an MBE in 1960' Foreign Office Statement of Services 1964

'she remembers meeting Hester' Email correspondence with family